PITBULL BOUNCER!

A Proven Guide for Nightclub Owners, Bar Managers and Security Personnel!

Gabe Cohen & Dave Gerber

TESTIMONIALS

"Gabe Cohen takes the role of a "bouncer" and redefines it for the modern world. Going far beyond the title, this book was a great culmination of philosophy, best practices, strategy, communication, relationships and reality. While the old definition used to create the vision of a huge dude manhandling "bad" clients in a bar, this perspective uses Gabe's successes as the new standard...which required far more than just being a Pit Bull. Great job Gabe and Dave for bringing this book to life!"

>Bram Frank,
>Founder-Grandmaster CSSD/SC
>Founder Modular Tactical Systems
>Grandmaster Conceptual /Combat Modern Arnis

"Gabe Cohen's unorthodox background and his devotion to the art of Krav Maga set him a world apart from the studio trained hobby martial artist. His consummate skills and keen intellect at both conflict prevention and resolution have made him an invaluable asset to Bootsy Bellows Aspen. For any business owner in need of security services, this book is a must read."

>Alexander Verus
>Floor Manager, Bootsy Bellows Aspen

"Gabe Cohen is a highly dedicated and driven man. His students past, present and future are lucky to have him as their trainer for self-protection...specifically in Krav Maga. This man is constantly training to improve himself so that he can improve others and no matter the financial cost to him. I will always be in this man's corner. If you can, seek him out and train with him!"

>-Bob Trotter,
>Chicago Police Officer with 12+ years,
>(Superintendent's Award of Valor, Lifesaving Award, and the F.O.P Distinguished Service award)
>1st Degree Black belt in Tae Kwon Do, Instructor
>Wing Chun Gung Fu
>Krav Maga Force Training Instructor & Krav Maga Civilian Instructor
>Certified Woman's Self Defense Instructor
>Certified Mixed Martial Arts Conditioning Coach

"This is a professional's approach to managing people, use of force, and violence from the perspective of someone who has walked the walk. Gabe Cohen's subject matter expertise goes beyond merely working the doors and racking up war stories. His thoughtful approach to both his security work and his Krav Maga business stands out because it is professional, purposeful and intelligent. This book captures every bit of that and more. Anyone in this business needs to have a copy as it is comprehensive, provides valuable information that can be applied immediately and is a great read!"

Scott Mitchell, Provident Personal Protection

"As a DJ who has worked in the bar, nightclub and private event industries for over 20 years, I can attest to the hard and unpredictable situations that can arise if the proper security measures are not taken. Gabe's professional and diligent approach works, and should be considered as an industry standard and a 101 to anyone getting into the industry, or anyone who has been in the industry. Using these methods, owners, patrons and staff can rest easy (and completely focus on their work) knowing that they will remain safe, at all times, while still providing and enjoying a fun and exciting atmosphere. As an entertainer, our safety is a must, and Gabe has always made sure we've had that in and around the DJ booth."

DJ Naka G (X Games, Olympic Games and DJ to the elite)

"There is no one that can lead and do the security work like Gabe. Every shift he was working there was a greater air of confidence about our overall security and personnel safety – literally, everyone on the team knew we were in very capable hands. This book brings it all together and was an awesome read for both me and my husband!"

Holiday Anne Schaldach, Nightclub Cocktail Waitress

Pitbull Bouncer: A Proven Guide for Nightclub Owners, Bar Managers and Security Personnel

© 2019 by Gabe Cohen and Dave Gerber
Timeless Publishing ▪ All rights reserved (1/2019)
ISBN: 978-0-9788707-9-9

Special thanks to Pete Toborek from www.badassphotograpy.com for the cover photo

Special thanks to Ojedokun Daniel Olusegun for cover design and book formatting - Dannymedia47@gmail.com

Published by Timeless Publishing
www.TimelessPublishing.com

No part of this publication may be reproduced, stored in a retrieval system or transmitted in any form or by any means, electronic, mechanical, photocopying, recording, scanning or otherwise, except as permitted under code 107 or 108 of the 1976 United States Copyright Act, without the prior written permission of the Author. Requests to the Author for permission should be addressed to Timeless Publishing, 5617 Bellington Avenue, Springfield, VA 22151

E-mail: **info@timelesspublishing.com**

Printed in the United States of America

IMPORTANT NOTE!

This book has been written and published strictly for informational purposes only and in no way should be used to replace or substitute actual instruction from and with qualified professionals. Gabe and Dave encourage everyone to learn and practice self-defense with professional coaches and instructors!

The authors and publishers of this book are providing you with knowledge and information. If you choose to act on it, at your own risk/liability, we urge you to be aware of your legal rights and health status by consulting appropriate legal advice for your state and a licensed health care professional engaging in any of the activities described in this book.

Names have been changed to provide honest stories with anonymity for those involved.

GABE'S DEDICATION

To my sweet angel, my lovely wife Amy, who spent many sleepless nights wondering if I'd make it home safely…and, for having to deal with occasionally being woken up with me needing to go to the hospital. Thank you for soldiering up all these years and sticking by me. Much love!

Gabe
September 8, 2018

DAVE'S DEDICATION

As with all of my work, this is dedicated to my daughter, Jessie Leah Gerber.

This book is also dedicated to everyone trying to find their place in the world, to those who feel under-utilized by society, and to those who have devoted their lives to serving others, even at their own financial/physical expense. This is dedicated to my past coaches who helped me understand the critical distinctions of Krav Maga techniques and instruction. This is dedicated to the military, law enforcement, and all those that work hard every day to keep us all safe.

Dave
November 11, 2018

ACKNOWLEDGEMENTS

I am indebted to Imi Lichtenfeld (R.I.P.) the founder of Krav Maga (the English definition of the Hebrew words Krav Maga means Contact Combat.) I never had the pleasure to meet him but he has taught me so much about what it means to be Jewish. Krav Maga is so much more than just a fighting system created for the Israeli Defense Forces. It has been a bridge connecting people around the world interested not only in learning how to protect themselves and others but how to become humbly empowered to overcome obstacles that would stop the average man in his tracks.

I have had many great teachers over the years and I will continue to train with the best in the world in order to pass on the essence of this great man through his Krav Maga.

My grandfather, Ben Wartell, was stopped on a train by Nazi soldiers with forged documents to hide his Jewish identity. "If even one bead of sweat ran down my forehead, none of us would be here today," he used to tell us when I was a young boy. He taught me to work hard, never quit and to dream big.

I call Dave Gerber, my book coach and partner on this project "The Professor" for his deep education and unique ability to simplify the difficult whether it is writing or teaching people self-defense. He encouraged me to press on when life was getting in the way of my writing. I am grateful that our paths crossed. Thank you, my friend.

Special thanks are due to Andrew Sandler who gave me a venue to implement my strategies and tactics at his nightclub Bootsy Bellows Aspen. Once I learned that his father, Paul Sandler, was an American combat hero in Vietnam, having served with the 101st Airmobile Division, Pathfinder Group, as a Lieutenant and then the 10th Special Forces Group, was awarded the Bronze Star and 4 Air Medals for Missions performed, it was obvious where this man got his drive and we quickly became friends. It has been an honor and a privilege to be of service to you, sir.

Most of all I thank God for the three perfect angels he has blessed me with,: my sons, Austin, Alex, and Asher. It is with them that my sun rises and sets.   – Gabe Cohen

TABLE OF CONTENTS

Foreword.. 10
Preface... 13
1. Leadership & management philosophy........... 20
2. Strategy, Tactics, and Logistics..................... 38
3. Relationships with law enforcement............... 59
4. Teams, roles, and responsibilities.................. 71
5. Communication and Surveillance................... 84
6. Creating and using the physical environment..... 95
7. Working the door, creating the energetic, and keeping the peace............................... 109
8. Controlling physiology with verbal and nonverbal body language........................... 119
9. Hands-On techniques and separating fighting patrons....................................... 131
10. After Hours... 145
11. Conclusion.. 155
Afterword.. 157
About the Authors.. 158

FOREWORD

If any nightclub, bar, or similar establishment is going to be successful, it won't be just about how much booze is sold. It will depend on creating an experience that people can't get elsewhere but also ensuring there is the right security team capable of reducing all types of negative behaviors, potential lawsuits and other types of distractions …that is mandatory.

A lot of businesses in this industry try to get by and cut corners on security. From my experience, this is a big mistake. What is also wrong is not ensuring that everyone is properly trained, knows and practices their roles, and is led by a competent, proven leader. In this industry, one wrong move could mean a lawsuit; it has proven many times that it is mandatory to have the right people on hand to ensure patrons are safe, having fun and being respectful to people and property.

Gabe Cohen has proven to be one of those individuals that is willing to risk his own body to ensure safety and order is maintained. The amount of knowledge Gabe has brought to our nightclub business is enormous. From retraining the staff, to implementing basic tactics, to reducing incidents and ensuring positive outcomes Gabe has worked tirelessly.

It's always important to have appropriate fundamentals and counter measures when dealing with a bar crowd. Gabe's fundamentals for controlling rowdy patrons, protecting the VIP area and running the door successfully became staples in the club. Interaction with the crowd, civility and friendliness are hallmarks he instilled in the staff.

The Pitbull Bouncer, is a wonderful "How-To" guide to protecting your business, successfully managing a crowd, collaborating with police, the do's & don'ts, common mistakes and so much more. This is an outstanding book and it is in the best interest of every club/bar owner, manager and security staff member to own it, read it and live it.

–Andrew Sandler, Aspen Night Club Owner of the Famous "Bootsy Bellows"

> "Failure will never overtake me if my determination to succeed is strong enough."
>
> Og Mandino

PREFACE

Having been a bouncer on and off for over 25 years I have experienced many things. I wish I would have had proper training to better prepare me for this line of work but in the beginning I was just happy to have a job and was confident enough that I could handle myself in whatever situation presented itself before me.

I've never been sued or arrested but did have to answer once to excessive force charges. There is so much liability that rests on your decision-making doing this job as a bouncer. Eventually I would work my way up into a supervisor position where I was responsible for all security team members including armed doorman for several different nightclubs.

On one job the firm I worked for had 5 popular clubs on one city block. We had sometimes more than 25 people on shift; after last call when the bars let out we would have anywhere from 2,000 to 2,500 people in the streets. We had to assist law enforcement with crowd control.

On another assignment, I was in charge of the security team of a venue which was having its Grand Opening within weeks of the most popular nightclub in town getting shut down for too many violations of the law. In addition, the area had a rough reputation for troublemakers fighting every week. Our job was to set the precedent here. We had to get rid of the riff raff but stay professional. Needless to say we were going hands on every night for the first few weeks as the locals wanted to play tough guys and were testing us. This club needed a solid team because without a professionally trained security staff the chances for survival were very low. This is true regardless of the size of any establishment, but when you have 500 to 1000 people in one place drinking alcohol your security staff better have good training and an understanding of the law.

When you don't have a team it can be even more dangerous. At one point in my younger days I was a doorman and the only bouncer for several small local bars I was completely on my own with way too many things to consider and deal with…having a team, no matter how small, is always preferred as you know you have at least one person that has your back.

I wrote this book because I want to help people in this business be as safe as possible and "have their back!" Many nightclub owners and managers have good intentions and think they know what they need with respect to security. But there are few in this business that really have this experience and, because of their lack of security training and preparation, they are forced to learn costly and tough lessons. These "new" situations could put them out of business or out of a job just because of one bad security employee who wasn't properly trained. My hope is to encourage this preparation and training, regardless of how many team members you have to start.

Today, I am hired to train security staff and am a consultant for new and existing nightclub owners/managers/teams. I thought to myself that so many more people could benefit from my experience if I wrote this guidebook and made it available to the public.

Also, on an individual level, beyond management, I wanted to offer a personal connection for the guy wondering if he has what it takes to do this job **and** for the guy who is already doing it yet is mature enough to keep an open mind on how he can improve.

For any employer, manager or team member wanting to secure a successful future in this business…this book is written for you.

-Gabe Cohen

> "The more you sweat in peace, the less you bleed in battle."

General Norman Schwarzkopf.

My Reality: Working the Door

I hate working the door. Having to deal with the drunk people outside the club that you're not going to let in is not the most fun experience, to put it mildly. As you can imagine or have experienced, people don't want to take "no" for answer and there is nowhere for you to run and hide.

Inside the club it's easy to "act busy" and move from one spot to another to get away from annoying people. Sometimes you just can't leave your post for security reasons so you try to be as polite as possible to get these people that can't take no for answer to move out of your personal space. It doesn't always work out peacefully, no matter how hard you try.

Watching from inside of the club one night I saw a guy giving my two doormen a problem. The guy's body language said a lot and I also saw him leaning into them, talking with his hands, positioning one foot back as if getting into a fighting stance and more subtle movements. I saw all this in less than a minute. There is also a line so we have to stop the flow of people in the club waiting for people to leave to make sure we don't go over the legal capacity. Unfortunately, some people don't get this or don't care and sometimes in their drunken state feel a sense of entitlement, too.

Whatever the issue was I didn't know but after a few minutes I saw this man still there giving my guys a hard time in front of a line of well-mannered customers. This has been going on too long for me and I need to get this man to move on. Why my team members haven't taken the necessary steps to get rid of him I don't know but it was time for me to find out.

Apparently he was upset because he was told he had to wait for "x" number of people to leave the club before he could be let in. According to him my guys miscounted and he should have been permitted to enter the club by now. At this point, I asked him if he could calm down, take a few steps back and wait patiently like everyone else until the manager comes out and tells us we can let several more people in.

He says "no, I'm not moving!" I tell him to please step back and get in line or I am going to have to ask him to leave and won't permit entry into the club at all.

He steps up and gets right in my face. He raises his hand, pointing his finger in my face calling me an asshole and I say "please back up, you are making me feel threatened" and get his hand out of my face. He pokes me in the chest with his finger and I fire off what I call a warning shot, "One over the bow," with a final verbal warning.

This guy doesn't backup or lower his hands out of my face so I slap this dude, open handed, right in the face. Hard. That's my physical warning shot. Just a taste of what could follow at a speed which he never saw coming. My guys are shocked. Everybody is shocked.

"You're going to back up and not assault me again. I'm giving you the opportunity to get out of here before we call the police and they will cite you for trespassing." [You can see my handprint on his face.] I think he wants to talk but he's all choked up trying to hold back his tears as I see them welling up in his eyes. He is staring at me, now holding the side of his face and crying. Literally crying. He's sniffling and slowly backing up with a girlfriend tugging on his arm.

I turn to my doorman and ask, "You boys think you can handle this now?" and walk back inside. Within minutes a call comes over my radio. "Cops are here. We need you out front." I have to explain what happened because the guy called the cops on me. I tell them what happened. They tell me to "have a good night." The night continues…

"Leadership is the art of getting done, what we want done, because they want to do it."

Dwight Eisenhower

LEADERSHIP & MANAGEMENT PHILOSOPHY

Dave: Before we get to the subjects of the chapter, we all need to know…where did you get the name, "The Pitbull?"

Gabe: I think this is an important story to tell right away and I am glad you asked this up front. It is imperative for readers to understand that my experience as "The Pitbull" were from a time period in my life that does not reflect my everyday experiences, today. Before sharing how I have grown, who I am now and where I'm headed…I will answer your question.

I got the name "The Pit Bull" when I was in my 40's because of my take no nonsense and aggressive nature. "The Pitbull wasn't hired for his verbal skills," my boss used to say. I still needed a lot of training with my verbal de-escalation techniques!

When they hired me for one of my early jobs, I was originally told they didn't need me for two or three weeks. It was going to be the grand opening of a new club and they had that covered; but the boss knew inevitably that a few of his team, once put to the test, probably wouldn't work out. I had interviewed for the job after he had the opening shifts covered. Well the next day I got a call:" We had three fights last night. Do you think you can start tonight?" They called me in to regulate. I was more than eager to get started.

I had never worn a bulletproof vest before so when I arrived and he asked me to try one on I was wondering what I had just gotten myself into for only $13- an hour. I also needed to drive 70 miles each way to get there and back but this was an opportunity to build my resume. Security firms don't often hire convicted felons but sales is a numbers game and I had knocked on enough doors until I found the opportunity. My reputation was on the line.

Needless to say they were very happy with my performance and within a couple weeks I was promoted to a supervisor position. The bigger guys depended on their size to intimidate but most of them didn't want to get their hands dirty. Other guys were there only to look cool and try to pick up girls while others were big and full of charm but were banking on their words to keep them safe. Me, I was there to brawl. At that time in my life I still had a lot to learn and didn't know that there was more to this job then jumping into the middle of fights. But that's all I wanted at the time. That's all I had ever done in the past.

I was a tough guy for hire and felt that was the role I had to play. My lot in life. I was a an older guy, retired street thug, ex con looking for action on the right side of the law...not the type of guy I would hire today. Thank God someone saw the potential in me and was willing to take the risk to hire me and hope I could be trained properly. I was being groomed to manage the company but there was a lot to learn. You see, you can train someone how to use verbal skills, in customer service, tactics and strategy; but you can't teach heart. Or loyalty. Or instinct. Those are the characteristics I possessed that one soldier can recognize in another. My boss was a former law enforcement officer, a Veteran from the streets like me but in a different uniform.

My ability to go from 0-100 without hesitation coupled with my Krav Maga skills made me a huge asset... an aggressive, potentially dangerous Pitbull that needed to be kept on a tight leash. Because nobody wants a dog that bites...until they need a dog that bites!

Dave: Great way to start! So, what's on your mind as we roll into this subject?

Gabe: I have two main philosophies: 1) to lead by example, don't ask anybody to do anything you're not willing to do yourself. By setting the standard you help people reach their full potential. If smart and humble enough you will let them exceed your expectations and standards. Then, you and the ones you teach will grow into their full potential while you do the same. Its win /win and that my friend builds solid teams. And 2) I put the safety of my team members first. Sometimes I may have trained my team members more deeply but others don't have the experience or the confidence to make certain judgement calls…I work with them more. We need to be prepared for every situation and that starts at the top, with strategy, planning and anticipation. When I am working a room I am not only constantly scanning the crowd but also keeping an eye on all of my people.

Keeping track of team members is crucial even when you can't always see them, noticing their movement and making sure they are at their post. Everyone has a specific job to do and there is definitely a learning curve. With time, leaders will develop and deserved confidence will evolve. It is important to get everyone on the same page with standards and similar desire to improve. It will be the leader's responsibility to keep an eye on these individuals with less experience, skill and judgement.

Dave: What is "Top Cover?"

Gabe: This means that there are courses of action that are supported by management and leadership and this has to be provided all the way down the line from the owner or manager to the security team leader to his workers so that security team members can do their job without fear of every little thing coming back on them. As you like to say, Dave, "Eggshells have no business in the security business."

So here is an example and my philosophy and approach can address similar situations like it. Leadership has to share these with their teams and talk about how it is to be handled…again, getting on the same page. Sometimes I will see a patron, let's say he is trying to get into the VIP section where he is not permitted to go. One of my guy's with lesser amounts of experience will often engage this patron with too much conversation over the matter. It's pretty simple, "No means no." Of course we try to be as diplomatic, polite and respectful as possible so communication skills and a positive conversation are expected, to start. For example, "As much as I'd like to let you up here these are private parties and my job is to make sure only people who belong up here are in this section. So I'm just asking you kindly to respect me and the job I've got to do."

Leaders and team members can't get distracted. It is important to remember if working in a high volume club (with hundreds or even over a thousand people) you've got to be scanning and watching for trouble while securing your post and talking to the clients. Even if you are not occupied with a conflict, you often have to think about multiple things that are unrelated at one time.

You can't get sucked into a debate or someone else's drama while doing your job. It's an interruption and for the most part these people engaging you don't care about you or your job…so pay attention. If, after being kind they persist in trying to get their way, maybe not taking no for an answer, it may be time to step up your game with more "direct kindness."

Again, this is where a philosophy that is supported by leadership can be implemented in reality. Leaders and team members need to let patrons know these are not games, respect has been shown accordingly and now they need to back up rather than escalate. I make it known that "I need to pay attention to my job and that the leadership team of the club does not want me changing a policy for them." That might be followed up with me asking them to leave the establishment. Plain and simple. I have too much going on to spend any more time on this and leadership teams. Having a policy for dealing with these types of issues, practicing and role playing them out and looking for ways to reduce escalation is critical. And, a leader needs to be able to articulate what the policy is so team members can understand it "in practice."

With respect to this example I am working from here, if this patron doesn't move on at this point my policy is to radio in for back up. Team members want to have a "hands off" policy to start. When backup arrives, a team member can take over presenting a clean perspective that is supported by the original security member, like me.

When more back up arrives if this guy wants to argue or debate the same issue, then it's time for him to go. He can either show himself to the door or we can help him find it. We usually don't want the team member posted up at the VIP section to leave his post but if he does one of our "roamers" or a guy posted across the room can come cover his spot until he comes back. That's best case scenario and if everything goes smooth but everything is situational and

I've had to use my intuition to step in and handle the situation before my team member got themselves into a wreck.

This of course can have the ripple effect that gets friends of the trouble maker involved, which requires more security to get over there and it takes time. This puts more people at risk of getting injured, especially those compliant customers in the immediate range who are oblivious of what's going on.

Sometimes I can see these types of debates carrying on way too long and I can see a security team member uncertain as to what to do. This person might freeze up and just hope the problem will go away on its own. It usually doesn't and I watch the troublemaker become more aggressive and my team member getting frustrated yet stay passive. So when we talk about philosophy, we have to know why, how and when to escalate situations, starting from non-verbals and non-threatening language. That has to be the start, yet the ability to shift gears, demonstrate that you are willing to go "hands on" and engage physically may need to be presented…this is hopefully an occasional, unfortunate reality of this business. Those levels are situational and to be determined…but as far as an additional philosophy, don't get yourself or your men hurt. But you also have to know that the owner/manager has agreed in advance with all of the things you needed to do to carry out his policies.

Dave: Why is a strong leader important for a security team?

Gabe: Communicating the policies and proper procedures to the security staff and leading by example sets the ground work for a successful security team. Without proper leadership in place the vision for success is not clear. The security staff has a huge liability concern to keep the public safe and a strong leader can see potentially dangerous situations and set up preventive measures. This skill set often goes unnoticed but the true professional doesn't concern himself with accolades. Getting the work done with a smile should be the leader's only concern. This sets the stage for others to follow with pride knowing that the leader's interest is that of the club owner and safety of his staff. This type of healthy work environment makes for a fun and safe night out for the customers.

Dave: How do you ensure professionalism among your security staff?

Gabe: There are several things that are important right up front. Having proper screening and a formal application during the hiring process is the first set of expectations for any team that is going to be any good. Then, you need a very comprehensive, written security plan that covers every conceivable situation. You may need to update this plan when you find that you forgot something!

Next comes preliminary and ongoing training. Not just bullshitting through the motions…really trying to recreate what will happen in that club or bar later that evening. This is really important and leads to the next subject I want to mention.

Creating team building opportunities inside and outside of work is really important. Relationships will save lives and get people to go home at night with fewer injuries. A cohesive staff that works well together and shares common goals that are discussed and written out and lived to every shift…that's good stuff!

Dave: So with that in mind, what do you look for when examining the qualities of leaders for security supervisory roles?

Gabe: Well, let me list them as that might be easier:

- Integrity
- Adaptability
- Dealing with a changing environment
- Great communication skills
- Strategic Thinking
- Knowledge of the law
- Extremely high self-awareness
- Doesn't let money cloud judgement

- Ability to inspire
- There are many others

Dave: Who decides the philosophy of the management and leadership for the security staff?

Gabe: The owner of the security firm if it's a private company. Otherwise, the owner of the establishment and his management would create their own policy. The risk here is if they are unfamiliar with the laws. This could jeopardize the entire operation form the beginning. A lot of people might think this is common sense, but I have seen some people make basic errors around security and it cost them everything.

Dave: Is there a "pecking order" for safety within the bar or club?

Gabe: The first is to protect oneself; the next is to protect team members and then the patrons. Then it is to protect property. It is really that simple and in that order.

Dave: What are some of the biggest mistakes you see amateurs making in this industry?

Gabe: Having security staff members who are allowed:
- Poor hygiene

- Poor dress
- Overly aggressive
- Not aggressive enough
- Not decisive
- Not backing up other team members
- Presenting little confidence or presence
- Lack of shift preparation
- Not setting a positive tone at the door
- Underestimating a patron's skill set
- Not establishing positive relationships with the police

Dave: What happens if there is poor leadership?

Gabe: Bad leadership makes for an unsafe work environment, period. Also, this creates:

- Lack of safety
- Little consistency
- Team breakdown
- Lack of accountability
- Good people leave
- Inconsistent support levels
- Low morale
- The lowering of standards

Reality: "Settle down"

I was three steps up above the main floor, posted up at the VIP section making sure no one came up those steps that didn't belong up there and getting rid of anyone that got up there that wasn't welcome by the host of the private parties. I told this guy he needed to settle down. I'd been watching him for a while. Almost felt like he was trying to bait me as he was acting out immediately in front of me.

This guy had an athletic build, very similar to mine and a bit taller. He was acting obnoxiously, bumping into people and one patron even came to me to ask if I could do something about his behavior. My coworker had approached him in the middle of a busy crowd to give him a warning and the guy got in my team member's face.

He was not physically assaulting the bouncer but I could tell from his expression on his face and his posture that he was preparing for a confrontation that could get physical. I flew off my top step into the crowd and made my way (just a few feet) over to my coworker and this unruly patron. My security team member assured me that he had it under control, that the guy could stay if he'd just settle down a bit. I didn't agree with his decision, thought he was being soft and knew this troublemaker was not going to comply. You could see it by the attitude he was displaying and I could tell he wasn't intimidated by my coworkers warning.

As my coworker walked away the patron was standing there still staring at me. I got in his face and told him, "Look man, we want you to have fun tonight but you have to be considerate of other people. He seemed to change his composure to almost looking meek and said, "I promise you I'll be good."

"I don't know what he told you but I'm telling you I'm not playing around. I'll kick you out of here if I see you bump into one more person. I know you know what you're doing so please be cool…my colleague is not the one you need to worry about." Serious, firm, no smile. I wanted to get across that this wasn't a warning but a promise. It's important with guys like this one because they need boundaries. They are bullies and used to people being intimidated by them. Sometimes when they act meek to a real threat, other times that behavior is just an act, sometimes they slightly withdraw to build up courage to come back at you head on. They want to see if you understand the game, or stupid and they can play you.

[I've dealt with enough knuckleheads to know the psychology going on during this incident and know enough to always nip this in the bud because either way this guy wants to fight or he's going to make you work to get him out of the club. If he doesn't pass out or leave on his own this guy isn't leaving without some type of struggle. It's an ego thing. He came here looking for a fight and now he is embarrassed that he was told to behave.

As the security lead, kind of like a rodeo clown, I read the situation and come up with the best solution to distract the raging bull in order to keep others safe. Sometimes that means calling the bullies bluff and sacrificing myself for the colleague who otherwise would have been "punked" and most likely-receive a serious cheap shot from this troublemaker.

With guys like this, you "call them out" and they either try to fight or "bitch up." If they "bitch up" you have to keep your eye on them because you know they are fueling the fire inside their head and it's not over if they think they can get one by you. They will often keep their eye on you and when you're not looking they'll take it out on somebody they're confident they can beat down and usually have their escape route planned.

Sucker punches are common with these guys and you got to keep an eye on them once you have a verbal confrontation with them.
I usually do my best to make eye contact with them whenever possible to let them know I'm watching and waiting for them to do something stupid. Usually, I can make them so uncomfortable from across the room that they leave on their own. The bully gets bullied and as much as that sounds unprofessional it's for the common good of the entire establishment and totally professional in my book (which this is!) I'm there for my size, skills, experience with situational reading and response ability. I've created my own tactics that are really just behaviors adopted from the streets, from being incarcerated, from being in survival mode and from watching countless verbal, non-verbal and violent encounters.

But everything is situational and even the best laid plans are subject to Murphy's Law. In this business you have to expect the unexpected. Be prepared to be called out on your "game" and ready to back it up without hesitation. You learn that even the best of us freeze up, even if it's just for a heartbeat. At that point, everything that you've been teaching and preaching, your supposed expertise in this field suddenly comes full circle to test you.

This is where the rubber meets the road and you get a fresh taste of the fear, wonder and awe that only being in the midst of a violent confrontation can bring. Where chaos unfolds and you are put to the test. When you feel the imminent danger of getting hit, injured or killed in a flash but it seems like minutes and then you realize what's going on inside you both psychologically and physiologically. That is the moment of truth when you either fold or fight and if you're a professional you remember who you are and in that instant, without hesitation, your training kicks in to full gear.

You act accordingly and take the fight to them. It's a beautiful moment and you can forever go back to that place in your mind, as I do often, to experience the fear and triumph of responding in a way that makes you feel proud because you know all that hard work you've put in over the years training was for moments like these. You are willing to be in this "arena" not knowing who your opponent or opponents may be or what the circumstances might look like. It doesn't matter, we signed up for this not for just the money.

No. That wasn't the payoff you were looking for when you committed to serve with diligence. You know that this moment is in fact your reward and next is your pocket change. It was never about the money, it was about the tests to see if you were in fact battle ready and worthy. Where winning isn't guaranteed and second place could mean death or a trip to the hospital.

That was my favorite flavor and although my tastes have changed with age I can still enjoy reveling in that moment as I write this and use those experiences to help others make sound decisions that can be the difference between their life or death. It's a very sacred thing and not to be coveted but shared to help the next guy survive.]

A little later…

Back on my perch, three steps up above the dance floor and main bar, the guy in question is acting up again. Although now he has a partner in crime and they got their arms around each other but interesting enough as they sway to the music together bumping into other patrons in this crowded nightclub his back is to me.

There are some tables with booths behind him which I am looking down from my post and see disaster waiting to happen. Thinking it's just a matter of time until they take too many steps back or bump somebody into the table (which very often has a bottle or several bottles costing the customer thousands of dollars I decide to act.) As I begin to step down the first step I see the guy I already warned literally fall back with his head just inches from smacking into the corner of the table behind him as he hit the floor. I get down there as soon as possible and clear the people standing around him out of my way.

"Are you hurt?" I ask, bending down to see if he's conscious.

"I'm o.k.," he says.

"I'm going to help you up and escort you out of here, O.K.? It's time to go." I lift him by his hand and arm to help him up onto his feet. He doesn't say anything at first and is compliant so I just keep my hand on his arm as I walk a step behind him and off to his side. He's heading towards the entrance on his own but then he turns into me and says, "why do I got to leave?"

"Dude, you fell over in the club. It's time to go," I reply. Just then as I try to lead him closer to the door and get him turned around to walk with me I feel somebody grab me by the arm. "What the f--k do you think you're doing?" a large somewhat overweight man that is taller than me by several inches asks.

I break my right arm free and shove the big man back to create some distance but as I do the guy I'm escorting out turns and violently grabs my shirt shoving me. As I begin to turn to regain my stability the big guy grabs me too and somehow I get driven several feet and my back hits the railing of the upper level, my feet stopped by the skirted wall around the upper level and in the moment I remember thinking, "F--k, this is going to hurt."

It's then that the back of my neck hits the upper railing and inside I'm cringing because in my mind I'm not sure which one it's going to come from but I'm just waiting to get punched in the face. I remember thinking in that moment too that my neck could snap if they use the railing as a leverage point (as I have in the past) to apply pressure on others to comply. Funny how all that goes through your mind in just a second or two and I remember it clearly. Next I recall seeing the rush of the crowd, not individuals but the total mass of close to 300 people moving in sync to see "the fight" and then I see one of my bartenders leaping over the bar.

That's when my training kicked in, "you snooze you lose" (i.e. he should've hit me when he could have) and I grabbed the first guy by his face with my hand and put one of my thumbs in his eye. This loosened his grip enough to where I could clinch on to the larger man and begin striking him with knees to his gut but it didn't do much to get him to back off. A very intoxicated ex-employee who I thought I was friends with got the patron who I was originally kicking out put in a choke hold of some sort. Not sure what happened to the other guy but I jumped up over my "friend" and punched the guy in the face because his arms were free and as I tried to gain control of him he was trying to hit me.

My "friend" then pushed me back, one hand landed on my neck. I told him to get out of my way and let me take this guy outside but he wouldn't let go of him and wasn't moving towards the door. It's my job to get him out so again I reached to get my hands on the troublemaker in order to gain control of him and escort him out but this time as I approached him this "friend" who came out of nowhere and threw a kick that just missed my groin. I instinctively nailed him with a right hook to the temple. I remember it being an open hand slap but witness said it was a punch, regardless he let go of the patron, grabbed his head and hit the ground. Several people grabbed me as I told a fellow employee to call the police.

Next thing I know I'm in the foyer and the police are outside handcuffing the first unruly patron just outside the club. The front doors are wide open, there are several cop cars there and the crowd of people is watching the crazy events unfold. According to one friend I punched him in the face when he tried to restrain me (bad move on his part, you don't get in the middle of a pit bull doing his job. You might get bitten!) but I don't remember that.

Then suddenly I hear, "You want some of me motherf--ker?" It's the big guy and he's facing, right near me, when I notice I am standing right next to a stairway that goes down two flights. Danger.

I remember being disappointed because at this point I wanted to inflict damage if this guy attacked me again. I knew with this much warning that I would in fact be justified and able to hurt this guy but my position of being on the top edge of this staircase was a huge liability, especially with this guy's size and weight coming at me. So I had to settle for a defensive push kick to his chest to propel him backwards into the arms of a fellow security team member who wrapped him up and handed him over to the police to be arrested.

As always I was interviewed by the police and this time chose not to press charges against these two customers. They were just drunk and stupid. I was glad I didn't get hurt and training was a good experience. No need for those guy's to have to face criminal charges from me, while many would disagree. I think "they got theirs" and they were going to jail for disorderly conduct.

While this guy needed to settle down from the start, you just don't get this type of training in your average martial arts class. This is why I loved this job!

> "The essence of strategy is determining what not to do."
>
> Michael Porter

STRATEGY, TACTICS, AND LOGISTICS

Dave: These are really important topics, for sure. Do you have any stories that come to mind to kick us off?

Gabe: One guy was instigating a fight with another guy. The other guy wanted to engage and we got there in time to make sure it didn't go to blows. My security team member took guy #1 back over to his table as I escorted the other guy, #2, to his table. Separating them is the first thing to do. Then you hear each guy out to try to piece together what happened.

Next, you get together with your coworker and find out what he was told. Then if you decide both parties can stay you have to keep your eye on them because one or both may not want to bury the hatchet. It is really never over until both think it is over. Really, I have followed along behind people who don't even know because they think a confrontation is done. Dangerous.

So in this case, I tell the guy that I had escorted back to his table of friends that I understand the other guy probably was at fault for starting this by "bumping into him" and that I'll keep my eye on him. "If I see him try to start anything new I'll kick him out."

Then I go talk to the other guy and feed him the same line. "Yeah, the other guy overreacted to you accidently bumping into him and if he doesn't let it go, I'll kick him out."

In this case and others I strategically plan different ways to diffuse issues depending on the type of establishment, physical environment, size of patrons and other variables. In most cases I make them both believe I'm their ally but I don't really care either way. In my thinking, whoever starts a fight needs to get kicked out. This is a great way to stay safe, use logic and easy tactics that diffuse most issues.

Now with this story, after conversing with the clubs floor manager the story he witnessed was the reverse. Classic. And even more classic, the real offender was mean mugging the guy who wasn't interested in any conflict. With new data comes new decision-making and there is nothing wrong with that…remove the ego and make the change if needed.

Sometimes even that doesn't matter and no matter what tactics, tricks or sound thinking you are using, something will get in the way. When I told the floor manager that my team would escort the offender out because he would not leave on his own…the same floor manager told me not too. He said," That guy and the woman he is with practically pay this place's rent."

So unfortunately for the "victim of the aggression" he would have to go. Politics are real and money is the deal. There is an unwritten policy at this place that if these two guys attempt to go at it again we take out the one that isn't starting the trouble. We know better who is at fault for instigating it but in this case it doesn't matter. Just like sound tactics not making a difference because you are not allowed to use them.

I talk to my security team members working in this section and give them a visual image of what this situation is going to look like if it goes down. If these two go head to head again, puffing up chest to chest, one of my team members is going to begin to separate them from the middle, another is going to go to our high roller and try to get him to turn around and myself and another team member going to take this other guy (the one that really shouldn't be getting removed) out of the club. A few other team members would be present to keep this poor guys friends at bay and make sure they didn't try to stop us because in effect, it wasn't fair.

Dave: Great way to start this chapter! Let me follow up there, what do you think is the most important thing to watch when confronting a disruptive patron?

Gabe: Their hands number one. What is in their hands and what are they doing? A clinched fist is good indication a punch may follow. Tapping ones pocket or a certain area, especially around waistband, is good indication they are checking to see that a weapon is still in place. They want to be sure they are prepared to grab it and give away that it's there. Regardless, any sudden reach into their pockets is an absolute "Go hands on now" for me.

There are several other hostile forms of body language that are easy to recognize. Such as sneering or flaring one's nostrils, lowering ones eye brows, clenching teeth, leaning forward, sweating, breathing more rapidly, pupillary constriction and shifting to the balls of their feet. These are all examples of pre-violence indicators that you must see before they act.

Dave: What's the best posture for a bouncer confronting a hostile patron?

Gabe: I always like to get my hands up in front of my face or at least up in between my shoulders depending upon the level of threat I'm facing. Palms should be facing out to display a defensive non-aggressive gesture of just trying to understand what's going on as peacefully as possible all the while my hands are up to defend against an oncoming strike or for a preemptive strike if necessary.

Dave: When confronting an unruly patron what's the best strategy to talk with that person if he is among his significant other or friends?

Gabe: Never back anyone in a corner to start with, they will only come back at you. Try to get him away from his people and try to talk with him privately. Putting a man on "Front Street" with his friends or girlfriend/wife present is not a good idea. This cannot always be avoided but if possible you may want to say, "Hey man can I talk to you over here for a minute?" Then I usually start off by giving him a compliment and voice my concern. This usually allows him to save face and not feel defensive, more likely changing his behavior quickly. There is a lot of basic psychology that goes a long way with this job.

Dave: Good cop/bad cop tactics, tell me how you use this strategy and why?

Gabe: It is a psychological tactic primarily used by police officers in negotiation or interrogation. This can also be applied to getting a patron to comply with the business establishment's policy.

I can often see trouble brewing among testosterone alcohol fueled young men when I'm bouncing inside a club. Instead of being passive or reactive and hoping that nothing bad happens or waiting until something does I like to give these guys a stern warning. I need to let them know we're watching them but more importantly that we have zero tolerance for violence.

I can call one of my security team members to accompany me to approach the patron with a warning to settle down or be asked to leave the club. One of us is the bad cop, usually me and the other "good cop" who will "save" this guy from being kicked out of the club.

I may say something along the lines of "management has been watching you and has asked me to escort you off the premises." Usually this is met with resistance and a demand to know why. I may say, "It doesn't matter, you've been asked to leave so let's start heading for the door." Best case scenario is he leaves without incident and we eliminated a potential threat.

But in most cases, the "good cop" will step in and give him an explanation of the behavior that we see and that needs to change. He acts like he is his buddy and can get me to back off and chill out if the patron can see to it to settle down a bit. He explains that he doesn't have to leave, and that he, as the ally, will smooth me over. Reality is, we never planned on kicking him out we just needed him to settle down a bit. Works beautifully, most of the time.

Dave: Assuming it doesn't and you decide he has to go, when escorting a patron to an exit what is the best way to get them to cooperate?

Gabe: Usually, if we can talk to them calmly, the best bet is to have them understand we are being fair and reasonable; that we don't want any problems and if they could leave on their own accord that would be wonderful. Best bet for all of us. Nobody gets hurt or in trouble with the law.

Dave: What happens if they don't want to cooperate?

Gabe: Well that all depends on how they don't want to cooperate. We will give them every means possible to leave the establishment on their own accord. Then it's up to the management and company policy about how they might want us to remove someone from their business.

We have a Use of Force procedure that we teach in our training. It's very important that the security staff has this training so they do not exceed what is proportionate use of force to the threat. After exhausting all forms of verbal communication a light hand on the back of the patrons arm to escort him out may work. It's a good place to start.

Then, if they resist use force that is reasonable to the resistance, start with a wrist lock and then go from there. I have several tactics that start so subtle but can have me in full control in a heartbeat. The last thing you want is to take the patron down to the floor or have an all-out brawl in the middle of the club.

There should always be at least two security staff present for any removal and the more the better. Sometimes it takes four people, two on the patron one leading them through the crowd and the other watching their back as they do so.

Another extremely important policy point is that once they are removed from the club they are not to be allowed back in. The doorman must know this and uphold it. The last thing you want is a disgruntled patron coming back in and blindsiding you. Security must work as a team.

Dave: Is there a certain protocol or script used to "keep the peace?"

Gabe: I personally am big on verbal, improvised role playing during our training. There are very polite ways to ask someone to straighten their behavior out or to leave and we as professionals must know how to diplomatically, and politely with a smile, use our words to peacefully de-escalate situations. The thing is you never know what you're going to get and you as a security supervisor or team leader need to plan beforehand what your people may say and how they may react.

This is not only a great way to help individuals who work with you but also a great team building exercise. Usually a lot of laughs and we have great fun with this exercise and through constructive criticism coworkers help to build bonds among the team members.

Usually once they find words that are comfortable for themselves they tend to adopt these as an informal script they will use during their shifts.

Dave: Why do you like the role play exercises?

Gabe: Because just like working out or doing martial arts the more we practice and refine our movements the more natural these things just flow out of us. It's building neural pathways or what people consider "muscle memory" and rehearsing scripts and posture, stance, etc. It becomes second nature and that's what we want.

Dave: Do you show differential treatment to a very popular wealthy client, VIP, or friends of the staff, owner/manager?

Gabe: You know look, you got a guy spending $20,000 for private bottle service and he slips a hundred dollar bill in your pocket upon arrival you're going to go the extra mile for that guy. It doesn't mean you're going to let him bully the guy who only spent $10 at the bar. Every customer has the right to feel safe and be safe while they are enjoying themselves. That's primarily my job.

Here is an example. I make sure the owner's mother gets escorted properly through the crowd when entering or leaving the establishment and make sure she gets to the door safely when she is exiting, having my door guys watch her at all times. The owner of the club is my friend but I would do that for anyone's mother. I'm a sucker for high rollers, mothers and babies...don't see many babies in the club!

Dave: Is the "no hands on ever" policy a good one?

Gabe: That takes a very mature staff and the willingness to set yourself up to take a hit if you're not a highly experienced martial artist. Waiting to defend yourself before you can go hands on in a dark, loud, crowded nightclub takes a certain kind of person.

I'm not that person. It makes for a high turnover rate among security staff and since they have a no hands on policy they tend to hire more inexperienced people for the job. Then, God forbid something starts off requiring skilled people to handle violence then they are behind the eight ball big time. Possible worse lawsuit and doors closed.

A customer is unruly, uncooperative and a danger to staff and other customers and you must try to contain this person at the establishment while awaiting the local police response. Do you know what the average response time is in your city for local law enforcement to show up on scene? Somebody could get seriously hurt or killed in a matter of seconds.

Dave: Do you ever lie to the customer if it is for the greater cause of the well-being of the establishment?

Gabe: Absolutely. Most of the time these people are under the influence of alcohol, sometimes drugs or both and they are not thinking logically. They will talk in circles and even though you may be very fair and reasonable they don't get it.

I'll give you an example of when I am trying to get someone to leave that isn't a violent threat and really doesn't need to be physically removed but for whatever reason needs to go. I might use a very low tone while speaking or no sound will come out of my mouth on purpose and then I will make like I can't hear anything they're saying. I'll ask them to come outside with me to talk.

Once we get outside I tell the doorman not to let them back in and I just turn around and leave them out there. If I feel like giving them a brief explanation I may but usually we're so busy that I need to get back inside.

Dave: Do you profile your customers looking for potential troublemakers and if so, can you give us an example?

Gabe: Sure. Sometimes if we see a guy let's say wearing some type of mixed martial arts shirt we'll want to watch him extra close. If he is involved in any type of potentially violent situation we generally escort him out first. We don't know if he is a highly skilled trained fighter or not but we are not going to find out the hard way if we can help it.

We watch for all of the pre-violence indicators that I have mentioned, body language, track people and their energy, who is throwing stares…most people are there to have fun so trouble makers are not hard to spot. We might also look for gang affiliations, that stuff sticks out as well.

Dave: Can a lot of violent confrontations be avoided?

Gabe: Yes and this is one of the biggest things I stress in our training. Seeing potential problems and handling them peacefully in a very diplomatic manner is the name of the game, but again this comes with experience and training.

Dave: Then how come it's not done more often?

Gabe: Inadequate staff that is not trained to "see" what lies in the invisible. Or, maybe they are lazy, unmotivated or not paying attention to what's going on around them. Only reacting if and when something happens instead of putting out small fires before they get out of hand is a critical mistake. This is one reason why violence happens, because it wasn't stopped at an earlier level and point in time.

While it might be counter-intuitive for the reader, I squash a lot of potential messes by being positive when they might expect a big guy to start off negatively. Being proactive when I am working is important and I expect everyone on the team to do the same.

Dave: How does one train to do what you are sharing in the book?

Gabe: As you know from your own experience gaining an Instructor level black belt in Krav Maga, everything is about practice and desire.

Additionally, I have spent countless hours working in these nightclubs and bars. The training manual that I created to train my team and use to train others was carefully crafted from my experience. Researching, interviewing fellow security professionals, law enforcement officers and drawing upon my Krav Maga training helped shape my business and working training model.

Through hands on security training workshops, webinars and our manual we offer online support 7 days a week. You and I also offer training together, Dave, and you offer self-defense training as well on your own. Bottom line, you have to train!

Dave: You have mentioned the bottom line. Can a lower pay scale for staff lower the quality of people and training?

Gabe: Absolutely. Remember, you get what you pay for. Unfortunately an objection I often have is that a company doesn't want to spend money on training because they spend so much on insurance and believe that's good enough. Sometimes having this training in place can actually lower ones liability insurance rates. However having insurance isn't the answer to violence prevention every night at the club.

Lack of training, poor training, and inadequate security staff could put a thriving nightclub out of business. The public has every right to feel safe and they **should** be safe when going out, spending money that supports the venue and its staff.

Professionals will cost the employer a little more but the atmosphere and the results are worth every nickel. The nightclub or bar owner owes it to the safety to the public as a part of the service being provided so they can have a great time. The benefits also include that people are going to tell their friends about the fun and safe atmosphere. It's a win/win for everybody.

Dave: Economically speaking how do you justify the cost?
Gabe: One stabbing, one shooting, one death. Cops there every night arresting someone. The ambulance ever present is not good for business, wouldn't you say? None of these

things are good for business. Lady's purses disappearing. Poor social media reviews. All these things can put a club out of business. One overzealous, untrained bouncer seriously hurting or killing someone is not good for business. This is not a fear tactic. It is our reality based on facts, what I have seen and what everyone in the industry intuitively knows.

Dave: How do you determine the number of security personal for a specific location?

Gabe: Some venues try to use the simple rule of one security staff member for every 50-75 people but there are many factors that make this not the best method. Other factors to consider when trying to develop a good ratio are:

- The type of venue must be considered.
- Is it live music?
- What kind of music?
- The layout of the venue?
- How many floors does it have?
- Entrances? Exits?
- Do they allow minors with stamps or wrist bands?
- What is the general crowd like, etc.?

Also, how well trained are individual staff members and the team together as a unit. So, there are many things to consider.

Dave: What would you say is the common goal for all strategy, tactics, and logistics in this work if you had to summarize?

Gabe: The common goal is to protect the customers, employees and the establishment itself while providing a safe and fun atmosphere for the customers.

Reality: Who is the Bad Guy?

"Security to the DJ booth! Security to the DJ booth!"

The house lights came on and I was making my way through the crowd to see what was going on. I was expecting a brawl but as I approached there was no one fighting.

"What's up?" I asked the DJ.

He replied quickly, "Guy at the bar, passed out and bleeding."

The bar was just a few feet away and sure enough a guy is leaning against it, standing but slouched over with his head buried in his hands. With one hand gently on his right arm I ask him if he's all right. He lifts his head and looks at me in somewhat of a daze. He tells me he's all right and I notice he has blood on his hand. Not sure where he was cut but only his right hand was bloody.

[I had recognized the guy now from the night before. He had told me he was from out of town and I remember noticing his prison tattoos. The reason I remembered him is because I made it a point to keep an eye on him the night before. He had looked wired, high on something and his clothes hinted of urban city "gang banger", not common for this club, definitely out of place.]

So, I asked him how he got cut and he said he didn't know.
"Well, it's time for you to go. I'm going to escort you out to the front door. Can you walk o.k.?

"Why do I gotta to leave?" he tests.

Looking him in his crazy eyes, "You passed out and are bleeding on my bar. It's not open for debate, start moving." I kind of pulled him away from the bar, not roughly but trying to get his ass moving. He wasn't that big of a guy, average size, but I didn't want to get him in a wrist lock for the escort because I wasn't wearing gloves (remember, the dude was bleeding.)

I let him walk in front of me as I kept my hand on his arm as we made our way through the bar. About half way through the crowd he flips the hood from his hoodie over his head. Seeing these types of odd, erratic or out of place behaviors is an immediate waning sign.

[Why cover your head in this hot nightclub? Was he about to get violent and thought he should try to cover his identity? Was he worried about witnesses and cameras? Mentally I went onto the next level of heightened security.]

I was watching his hands and getting ready for a possible attack.
Then sure enough he reached his hands into the front pouch like pocket of his hoodie. "Get your f--king hands out of your pockets!" He tries to break loose of my grip on his arm and I don't know if he's got a knife or a gun but I'm not going to wait to find out.

I shove him face first into the closest wall and yell again to "get your hands out of your pockets" but his hands remain where they are. Instantly I under-hook his arm, grabbing him now from the back with both hands. I take him off the wall and face plant him onto the floor. I wrestle his hands out of his pocket; he's bleeding now from his face.

My coworker comes to my side. I tell him that he reached in his pocket and might have a weapon but I got him. "Move the crowd back and I'll take him out the door." Still on top of this guy who is face down on the floor I say, "Can you breathe OK?" He says he can and then I tell him I'm going to help him to his feet and get him to the front door. Not to resist or I'll take him to the ground again. "Do you understand?" He says he understands.

I lift him up to his feet and notice a bag with a white substance in his right hand. Probably a bag of cocaine but I'm not worried about that at the moment. At this point I just want to get him out the door. As I get him pushed through safely I release him and tell him to get lost before the cops show up. He takes about three steps in the other direction but then turns violently and swings on me. I duck, pop him in the face, step into him and hip toss him face planting his already bloody face into the concrete. I transition into an arm bar, knee in his back and let him "if you try to resist, I am going to break your arm."

I notice the bag of coke (I'm assuming) is no longer in his hand. "Call the cops," I tell my doorman. Another bouncer is standing above me. I look at my colleague and say, "here, come get this guy. I'm going back inside to wash my hands. Come get me if the cops want to talk to me." Apparently the guy was snorting coke that was on a keychain he was holding at the bar. He passes out and somehow cuts his hand on one of his keys. That's when the DJ called me. Because some people don't understand or see what happens in a split second or get to watch me defend myself and other patrons with aggression, I'm the bad guy!

> "We must honor, protect and support our police officers and their families every day of the year."
>
> Janet Reno

3

RELATIONSHIPS WITH LAW ENFORCEMENT

Dave: You must have some good stories that include law enforcement, where do we start?

Gabe: Most law enforcement officers are good people, trying to do their job and go home alive. I respect that. It is important, like with anything as you know, to build good relationships. With this type of work it is especially important. So my first story might not be what you think.

I locked my keys in my car one night and didn't realize until the end of my shift. I was tired, it's like 3 a.m. and I just wanted to go home. Calling a locksmith is going to be at least $100-$150 that I was not looking forward to spending.
One of the local cop's was driving by and saw me out on the street shining my flashlight in my window looking at my keys on the front seat.

"Locked your keys in the car Gabe?"

"Yup."

He pulled right over and had an entire kit for opening car doors. After several attempts he got the door open for me and I was on my way home.

Really made my night and I had so much appreciation for that man and his job. I didn't even know his name when he arrived but he knew mine. They'd been called several times to our venue and I was usually in the midst of why they were there. It was nice to know that my reputation as a professional proceeded me.

Dave: Excellent, good story, positive and demonstrates reputations and relationships. What are the benefits of a good working relationship with local law enforcement when working club security?

Gabe: The benefits are that these are the people that you rely on to get your back if things get out of control. They have a lot more tools and officers at their disposal. Hopefully you'll never need that type of serious assistance but if you do it sure is a relief when they show up!

Sometimes it could be a single individual that is breaking the law in some way at your establishment or several individuals. They need to be held legally accountable for their actions which upholds the integrity of the establishment. It lets the public know that you have zero tolerance for illegal activity on your premises.

Most importantly is that the men and women who serve and protect us who work in law enforcement should be honored. Security teams can do that by showing courtesy and respect while doing their job. Handling what they can on their own and assisting law enforcement officers if the need arises. It's win/win for the entire community when we all work together with the common goal of keeping people safe.

Dave: How do you establish this rapport?

Gabe: As a manager for a security firm you need to go down to the local police station and ask who the sergeant is that oversees the area your bar or club is in. Introduce yourself, ask if there's anything you can do for them and if there is anything you need to know about (such as drug or gang issues). Ask who the patrol officers are during the shift when you will be working and ask for their cards.

I am also certified as a Law Enforcement Officer Krav Maga Instructor, have my black belt in Krav Maga and teach throughout the United States. So I usually offer some training opportunities to them at a discounted rate and usually comp the LEO's that patrol my venue if they are interested.

I tell my staff to build a rapport with them when they show up at the club. Be friendly and respectful as they should be to everyone.

Dave: What are the pros and cons of having LEO's (Law Enforcement Officers) show up at the venue on a regular basis?

Gabe: I like them coming in to see what's going on now and then. A friendly greeting as you welcome them into the venue speaks volumes to the customers. People want to feel safe and we set up an atmosphere that lets them know we take our job seriously.

The benefits would be
- Demonstrate connection to law enforcement
- A lawing abiding establishment
- Pro-active to ensure security for customers
- Connected to customer service
- Connect with the larger community as an upstanding establishment.
- Not afraid to have the police in your place

The cons would be:
- Having police cars in front of the club sends up a red flag that can leave people creating their own story
- Some people don't like police
- Customers might not believe it is safe because the police must have to be there to babysit.
- Could affect alcohol sales because they may feel it is an uptight establishment

Bottom line, the pros out way the cons and it is definitely beneficial to have a good relationship with the police and the community.

Dave: When should security or management call LEO?

Gabe: There are many reasons that security may call the police, from underage drinking to assault. If somebody breaks the law my policy is that we notify law enforcement.

However you don't want to call them to handle things that your security staff can and should do on their own. Law enforcement stay busy with very serious calls at times and you don't want to waste their time. It's disrespectful and unnecessary.

It's about a balance. The other thing is having frequent police presence may be bad for business because the public, who may not know why they are there, may have the perception of constant trouble at this place…maybe it could be dangerous and that the security team doesn't have it under control. You have to consider the public's perception to seeing three police cars, lights flashing every time they go past your club or entering it. Not good.

You call when necessary like if there's a fight and someone gets hurt or one party wants to press charges.

Dave: Should security staff have one designated person for calls to local law enforcement?

Gabe: Everyone on my security staff has the local police department's non-emergency phone number on speed dial and that is probably the only thing they would use a phone for on shift. Usually whoever is the supervisor will determine if police contact is necessary.

I have been in the middle of breaking up a fight that was just out of hand and yelled to a team member to call police. We needed more backup and these guys needed to go to jail.

Dave: Should the club owner, manager, or security supervisor/owner of Security Company be notified immediately after staff has contacted the police?

Gabe: Absolutely. A good security firm has attorneys ready 24/7 and an incident report must be written properly. Training on what to say to the police and what not to say is important especially if a staff member is being charged with something. Remember, even though you think you're "fighting the good fight" the public's perception, usually clouded with intoxication from drugs and alcohol can make for pretty damaging testimony against you. This is why having high quality security cameras is so important.

Dave: Is it best to deal with a higher ranking police officer on shift or should security build rapport with as many law enforcement officers as possible?

Gabe: The security supervisor should be the one dealing with law enforcement but those staff members involved in the incident will also be questioned. The supervisor should be present as much as possible. How we articulate our side of the story is most important. And, yes, rapport must be built with all law enforcement officers because we are fundamentally looking out for the same interests, peaceful fun for customers.

Dave: As security supervisor/manager did you ever get preferential treatment from law enforcement?

Gabe: Not anything outside of the law but establishing rapport with LEO's allows the officers perception of you being "fair and reasonable" helps when you have a crowd of intoxicated witnesses stating otherwise. I've had several incidents over my career where the officers actually "coached" me on how to articulate myself through casual conversation after an incident to help me learn how to do it better next time because they knew I was right; they just knew how the system worked. I have learned a lot from law enforcement friends over the years and am grateful.

Dave: In what ways can a club's security staff be an asset benefiting local law enforcement?

Gabe: I've worked clubs and bars in high crime areas where the police have shown up with photos of suspects they were actively looking for on a case. This is good information to know because if that suspect shows up he could be a threat to the entire establishment. One hand washes the other.

Is it a good idea to ask law enforcement their average emergency response time?

Gabe: Of course. I worked several security post's where our doorman were armed so the threat of violence was real…just as the need for backup. No matter how good they are, they can't teleport so you had better know how to handle the environment.

One private club was in an industrial type neighborhood that wasn't as busy as the downtown clubs and there was a heavier police presence. Before we got the contract they had three shootings in the parking lot in the first two months of business. The police response time was not that fast and the gang element knew it.

Dave: Other thoughts on the subject?

Gabe: As stated above, you want to know how long it will take to have police on scene, especially for those bidding on a security contracts as well as nightclub/bar owners. You need to have the right security in place with the right weapons if need be, even if they are "improvised" but you know where they are and how to use them to defend yourself. Cash walkouts with armed guards are highly recommended for high risk neighborhoods. Calculating response time helps determine the risk factors and other issues that need to be addressed in planning and training.

Reality: Assist the Police

Assisting the police was something that was very familiar to us on one of my security posts. It was a military town, one of the largest U.S. military bases in America. The firm I worked for had five nightclubs whose security we were responsible for every night.

The city had your average drug and gang problems too. At 2am you would have cops present trying to manage about 2000 people in the streets outside the clubs in front. I was an inside guy so until everyone was out of the club at the end of the night I didn't have to get involved with what was going on outside the club.

On this one night as my team members and I are herding the crowd to the front door I noticed all hell broke loose outside the club. There were big windows behind the front bar that overlooked our gated patio and the street. Total chaos and I noticed two of our guys go running off in one direction. Then I saw a lone cop on the street trying to get a guy into custody. They were on the ground and the man was resisting. It seemed the suspect had a few friends around and I felt the officer was in danger.

I ran out the patio door from inside the club and hopped the railing as graceful as an Olympic hurdler. There was total mayhem in the streets and as I approached the police officer who was trying to handcuff a resisting suspect it was obvious he felt threatened by a man who was standing over him yelling at him.

'I'm here to help you sir," I shouted at the top of my lungs. The smell of O.C. spray was in the air. This stuff is not fun to breathe as overspray was always an issue when that stuff is deployed. Essentially at the same time I just tackled that guy in the street, landing on top of him just beyond the struggling police officer.
Raining down punches from a mounted position as the guy was trying to fight back. Then a kick into my rib cage knocked me off

and to the side of this guy. Blindsided by someone who wanted to rescue this guy I scrambled to my feet. Ignoring the pain (thank you adrenaline dump) I saw the guy who must have kicked me coming at me. On my feet now I shot out a right side kick taking out his knee followed by a hammer fist to the back of the neck. The guy dropped and it was only then I noticed two more of my team members coming to my side.

"You o.k.?," one asked me.

"Yeah but I need something to drink," I replied.

"Go inside and get something we got this," the other one said.

There were two more police cars on scene now and the crowd was dispersing as it tends to do when there's an increased presence of law enforcement. My ribs were bruised pretty badly and it would be a long drive home that morning. The cop would come in the club the following weekend to thank me. Apparently the guy I originally tackled was attempting to assault the officer when I intervened.

We had to constantly watch our backs working this location, especially when going to the parking garage at the end of the shift. We usually all met and parked together so we could all roll up and out of the club together as a team. I liked that several of our guys were armed too. Can never be too careful.

"Teamwork makes the dream work, but a vision becomes a nightmare when the leader has a big dream and a bad team."

John C. Maxwell

TEAMS, ROLES AND RESPONSIBILITIES

Dave: How do you create the best security for a venue?

Gabe: Hiring the proper security team is the "Achilles heel" to nightclub risk management. Every team member should be carefully screened and undergo security training that brings up their environmental and situational awareness.

Sometimes the most skilled martial artist or muscle bound individuals are not the people you want to hire. A business need people who are trainable and leaders must be able to notice potential red flags in the hiring process.

Staff members need to be able to identify different kinds of red flags when working. We can teach basic tactics if things get physical but much of our work is recognizing problems before they happen and handling them quickly and early, in a diplomatic, customer friendly way.

Communication of the venue's policies and strong leadership must be in place to ensure everyone on the team is on the same page. Through proper training a great security team provides the service necessary to keep people safe.

Dave: What are some team member's different roles?

Gabe: The doorman or door people provide crowd control outside a venue, making sure a place doesn't get overcrowded and checking identifications to make sure everyone is of age. They are also often the first impression of the establishment so they must be well dressed, groomed properly and provide big smiles with a generous greeting for everyone. Simply, they set the tone and help to reduce/eradicate problems before they would even begin.

Then we have people positioned at specific places within the club for proper observation and security. Also we usually have at least one "roamer" who travels about within the club and mingles through the crowd. If there is a VIP section, probably one person standing right outside of it to keep the entrance clear and to make sure no one else enters.

Dave: What do you look for when hiring new team members?

Gabe: Let me give you a list: Integrity, trainability, solid background check, interpersonal skills, good writing skills, drug screen, proper judgement, objectivity, dependability, emotional control, maturity, if they know a martial art, have they served in the military, are they physically fit, do they have presence, good surveillance skills and will they follow the rules. By the way, martial arts background or military may be a liability, depending on the person's temperament.

Dave: Do they all have the same basic skills or do they complement one another?

Gabe: I would like them all to have the same basic skill level and they must meet the standard criteria…obviously some will be stronger in different areas. So, realizing this we try to pick what we think are the most important skill sets with each individual and then determine how this will look in the team setting.

We certainly look for people that can complement one another but we must not rely on that as a standard because not everyone stays with the team or shows up 100% of the time. We have a responsibility to the owner and management to provide the best service possible and that can really be best achieved with a solid team.

Dave: What role does the security supervisor have in creating team building events?

Gabe: This is so important because helping team members learn more about each other helps them work better together to achieve your goals. It's all about relationships…in many cases it is similar to law enforcement or the military because we are putting our bodies on the line every shift. To do that for one another, you have to have cohesion, respect, and people that want to get each other's backs, all the time.

As the supervisor or manager this person must take the lead with implementing these exercises and do it regularly. It also shows the team that this person in the leadership position cares about them as a whole. They see that resources are being spent on training and they feel valued.

Dave: Can you give an example of what you like to do?

Gabe: There are many resources out there to find various team building exercises. Some that I like best are finding common thread among team members and active listening.
By breaking them down into small groups you can have them create lists of likes, dislikes, family situations, backgrounds,

etc. Using pairs, small groups and a combination of large group exercises is best.

I like to have them share a few things they learned about each team member that they have in common with them. This works best in finding out what their common threads are and have them share a little about their life experiences in a safe way. Even though many of these guys are tough, there is a private side that doesn't need to be pushed too hard.

Dave: Who has the most responsibility on a security team?

Gabe: The security manager who is directly supervising the team and who is responsible for reporting to the establishments owners/managers. That said, like you always say, everyone is a Risk Manager. We have to remember the difference between a leader and leadership…everyone can demonstrate leadership qualities!

Dave: What makes a good team leader?

Gabe: A great team leader has integrity, is fair, leads by example, does what he says he's going to do, is honest, praises improvement, strengthens and encourages team members, is respectful, is a good listener, sets the bar high for himself and his coworkers and most importantly has plenty of real world hands on experience in the security field.

Dave: How important is it for security staff to know local and state alcohol, drug, firearm and equal status laws?

Gabe: Vital to the survival of the business. It is critical they know them, and they know how they are liable…both professionally and personally. If you are ignorant of the law, you are jeopardizing the business and the patrons, your team members and potentially your own freedom. You can't break people's civil right. If you handcuff someone under the wrong pretenses you could get an abduction charge. You have no more rights as a security guard as they have as citizens, and you are not law enforcement. You must know what you can and can't do, period.

Dave: How does a dress code for patrons make a difference for security staff and the overall establishment?

Gabe: You are trying to set the standard for what type of establishment it is, what "class" of people you want to do business with. Gang colors, tank tops and other problems with dress can create much bigger problems. Bandanas hanging out of people's pockets could start a gang fight.

And that's another compliment to working with law enforcement, they will let us know about current crimes that could impact the club. Gangs have shot callers, they would get treated so well as a part of keeping their own gang members.

Dave: Did you have any kind of pre-opening checklist security staff had to go through individually or as a team?

Gabe: I suggest that every club or bar have a checklist for every employee and team they need to go through, not just security. But in this case, yes, a pre-shift meeting to outline who would be doing what. Then, when people had their roles, they could go over anything that needed to be addressed for that responsibility before the doors opened. This is definitely a best practice.

Dave: Very interesting, lots of variables to consider. Sometimes you can plan and things still happen, that's just part of your business. After talking about this for a while, any stories come to mind?

Gabe: I see a fight at the bar. I'm about 10 feet away, three steps up off the main floor posted up at the VIP section. Leaping from my perch I quickly make my way through the crowd. I see the bartender hopping over the bar. These guys are in mid-swing. I instinctively get behind the bigger of the two and put my hands over his eyes while pulling his head back and down.

Concurrently, I take his knee out from behind, sitting him down in front of me but as I go to control one of his arms into a lock I see there is company. I look up and see another guy coming at me about to swing as I stand up and punch him in the nose, kick him in the groin and jump back onto the guy I took down to the ground before he can get back up.

I put him in an Arm Bar next, I take him out through the kitchen and kick him out into the alley. Then I see the guy I punched in the face being escorted out the kitchen too. I return into the club to find the third party has already been removed out through the front door.

The bartender is back behind the bar. I'm back up on my perch. The music continues play. It doesn't miss a beat. This is the life of a security team leader or member…you have to love it or you have to get out. If it works for you great, if it doesn't, move on…no harm, no foul. Everyone needs to do what is best for themselves in life.

REALITY: Pitbull Wanted?

I noticed this kid talking to one of my security team members. I could tell from their body language that the kid was intoxicated and probably time for him to go. I walked over to offer my "assistance" if necessary but he said he had it under control...

Next thing I know the kid is coming my way. I am standing next to a stage that is elevated a couple feet above the main floor. A band had been playing earlier but they were finished for the night. I can't remember exactly what the kid was saying but he was talking shit, telling me how I must think I'm a real tough guy playing "rent-a-cop" and wondering what my problem is with him.

"I don't have a problem with you. What makes you think that?" I ask.

"Why you got to come over and see if there's a problem when I was talking to the other guy? You must have a problem with me."

He gets too close to me, into my personal space. I tell him to back up and move along as there is nothing to talk about.

"What's your fucking problem with me?" he persists.

"Listen man, you're drunk and I don't have time for this. I advise you to get away from me before I ask you to leave the establishment."

"For what tough guy?" he says.

"Look man, I asked you once to back up and now I am asking you to leave the premises. You're too intoxicated and it's time to go."

"I ain't going anywhere and you're not going to make me do shit."

"Really man? This is how you're going to play this! I am asking you to leave now for the second time. I've asked you politely twice and you're making me feel threatened standing in my face like this. If you don't leave now then legally your trespassing and I we can have the cops come get you. The choice is yours. How do you want to leave here tonight?"

At this point one of his friends shows up and is standing off to my right side. Now he wants to know what the problem is and I tell him to do his friend a favor and take him out of here. I say, "Listen man you came here to have fun right? Let's not turn a fun night into a bad night. Help your buddy here leave the club or I'm going to do it."

"You aren't going to do shit," says the guy who is still invading my space.

So now I up my game, "Listen motherfu--ker how do you want to leave here? With your friend? With the cops? Or in the back of an ambulance? Because I've seen people get stupid in here and not be able to walk out of on their own. I'll tell you right now you won't win. So back up, turn around and get the f--k out of here."

Then I feel a hand grab my right shoulder. I see it as a distraction, a possible threat to my safety and fling the friends hand off my shoulder. Right as I do that I feel a hand grab my neck. BAM! I smash the original troublemaker in the face.

He stumbles back and falls over onto the stage. I try to close the range between us but he starts bicycle kicking me, his back on the stage, he lands a couple good kicks. So I sweep his legs over, hop on top of him, getting my feet up on the stage. On top of him and with side control position.

He is resisting and I try to control one of his arms but he's flip flopping around. I drop an elbow into his face and a knee into his ribs. By then a fellow security team member is there to apply a proper wrist lock and begin the cuffing process.
When the police arrived an officer asked me if I knew any Ju Jitsu. I did not. Apparently the public's perception was that I was too aggressive.

There was a hearing in reference to that night in front of the alcohol board. I had defended my actions even though there were no criminal charges against me. At the end of the hearing the alcohol board shut the place down for a weekend and fined them $5,000.

Nobody wants a dog that bites until they need a dog that bites. The owners of the club kept me.

> "There is nothing inherent in active listening to prevent an emotional reaction or protect your buttons from being pushed. But pausing after listening and before you answer prevents your mouth from going before your brain."

Rory Miller

COMMUNICATION AND SURVEILLANCE

Dave: Do you recommend all security staff have radios to communicate with one another?

Gabe: Most definitely. It's the lifeline in the security business. Calling for backup when needed and also to communicate before going into a situation helps keep the security team members safe. There needs to be clear rules on how to communicate and really important, keep the line clear.

Dave: Where do security members go wrong when it comes to using radios?

Gabe: They need to be as professional as possible. Short and to the point. Facts and no small talk. The radios must stay open for business only matters which includes emergencies. That's it, nothing more. People want to have fun with these toys…it's not a toy and extra chatter just gets in the way of safety.

Dave: How do you conduct training for this?

Gabe: We use the radios themselves for hands on training and do some classroom work on proper communications etiquette.

Dave: Are there dues and don'ts for on the air communication?

Gabe: The big thing is no horseplay. I had these two security team members joking about a fight on the bottom level of a two story nightclub. Sometimes it is hard to hear over the radio and crowd. All I heard was "there's a fight" and I went rushing through the crowd, down a flight of stairs, and was furious when I found out that they were just joking.

Dave: Some people don't want stuff caught on film, should night clubs and bars have security cameras as an absolute rule?

Gabe: Of course they should, it's not a matter of if, it's a matter of how good. The system helps to protect the public, the establishment and the staff. It holds everyone accountable for their actions. Simply relying on the public's perception for eye witness accounts is not the wisest thing to do in any town.

Also, if the security team does anything out of line the evidence will be documented on the video surveillance. This helps owners and management make sound decisions on who to keep employed and who to let go. Look, when it comes down to the public's safety and liability, the video does not lie. We need to deal with facts not opinions or the best of someone's memory.

Dave: What are the pros and cons of security cameras and surveillance?

Gabe: I am in the opinion that the pros outweigh the cons. Usually the public only sees the actions of the bouncer after he is reacting to a certain situation. People do not see what led up to his actions and it can often be misconstrued for overreacting or being overly aggressive.

Opinions are formed, attitudes are adopted and witness statements are often quite biased against the security staff. Let's not forget the influence of possible drugs and alcohol which can make for a very unclear perception of the facts by patrons. Security cameras tell the truth.

The cons of having security cameras is if you run an establishment where clients want to feel free to indulge and enjoy themselves without the potential of evidence being used against them (law enforcement can subpoena the surveillance footage)…especially if you have high end VIP or celebrity clients who may also worry about certain footage getting out into the tabloids. So in a sense it is a way for certain venues to use the fact that they don't have cameras as a selling point to attract celebrities and other public figures.

Dave: Where should these cameras be located? Both inside and outside the club?

Gabe: Yes, if you're going to have cameras then they need to be strategically placed to cover as much square footage as possible which the club/bar is responsible for. Some venues you are responsible for a certain number of feet outside the door. You must consider parking lot safety, too, if it applies.

Also it depends on the owner's and management's motives for these cameras. They can also benefit overall security to prevent robbery and theft. I've seen cameras positioned over the registers at the bars too.

Dave: If the surveillance cameras are known to the public

what areas may have blind spots and are these considered more dangerous than areas which are not under surveillance?

Gabe: Bathrooms for one are not under surveillance so these are definitely areas you want to watch your back. As you might expect, these are more dangerous to both patrons and staff.

Dave: Why and how could they be dangerous?

Gabe: Bathrooms are an obvious place to use and sell drugs. Unfortunately they have been used to ambush people that were unsuspecting an attack. The worst part about such an attack is unless there are witnesses the victim could be seriously hurt inside the bathroom for a while before security or anyone else for that matter are aware of it.

I have had disgruntled patrons follow me into the bathroom and came close to having to fight my way out. On another occasion I had caught several guys doing drugs in a bathroom stall, called for backup and we had an all-out brawl on our hands.

Dave: Did you have a policy about staff and cell phones?

Gabe: They couldn't use them while on shift, simple.

REALITY: Coat Check and Moving On!

I'm working my post in the VIP section. It's a live upscale music venue but the show is over. I get a call over the radio to go post up with another security officer at the coat check. "Ugh," I sigh, I never worked it before but from what I witnessed it's a pain in the ass.

You got a couple hundred people in a small venue, drunk, who all want to get their coats and get out of there at the same time. Our job is to get them to line up in an orderly fashion and keep the line moving as quickly as possible. No messing around, flirting, or arguing with the coat check girls. People get extremely impatient.
Then, of course, you got that random guy who wants to cut everybody in line because he feels some sense of entitlement to go before everyone else.

"Excuse me sir, the back of the line is down there. These people were here first."

"No, I was here."

"No sir, you were not. I'm asking you nicely to please go to the back of the line like everyone else."

This is tough and highly stressful as people's arms with their tickets for their coats are reaching over you, everyone trying to be next, regulating the line while dealing with one person who doesn't want to comply.

Then I realize we kicked this guy out the night before. Somehow he weaseled his way past our security officer posted up at the entrance that leads to the Green Room where the bands hang out before or after show time. I remember because it was at the end of the night and the band had no idea who this guy was and sent someone down to get him out of there. I remember he got very smart with me and wasn't violent but wouldn't move. I had to back down and ask one of my team members to take over when they showed up on scene because I was ready to start hammering him.

Fast forward to this night, there were no cameras or witnesses and he was saying some pretty disrespectful things. I've dealt out some back alley justice over the years but with age and maturity have learned to simply walk away when able. He is still giving me a hard time at the front of the cost check line.

I already know he's going to be a problem. Every time I turn around he'd cut the front of the line. I got him to remove himself from the line with consistent debate but this last time he basically bumped me to reach over and give the coat check girl his ticket. She took it without me realizing it as I turned to see who bumped me. The scene is quite chaotic.

He reaches for his coat as she hands it out to him but I tell her to keep it because he was not next. The people who have been waiting patiently appreciate it but this guy starts verbally abusing me. I make the judgement call to remove this guy so I grab his arm, apply a wrist lock, he immediately resists and I push him face first into the wall. I radio the door guy to come remove him so I can post back up to regulate the line.

He relieves me, takes the guy to the door but then instead of kicking him out he allows the guy to start screaming, starting a scene that I laid hands on him for no reason. He wants to press charges.

The owner comes over to hear him out, then tells him to wait outside the club for the cops and to leave. He won't leave, he says "I'll wait in here until the cops come."

The owner tells him he'll call the cops but he must leave the club now. The man refuses, the owner tells the box office girl to call the cops. Then he tells me to come over to the side to speak with him.

"We have a no hands on policy. If you touch one of my customers again, if you don't go to jail tonight, you'll be fired. Do you understand?" He didn't say it nicely and was telling at me like I was a kid. This of course didn't sit well with me. The cops came, they let the guy go, watched the video and didn't arrest me. I still had my job.

The next night was a rap concert of a famous artist who had been arrested before on gun charges. They wanted me to work the stage. I broke up a fight that night without hurting anyone and thought all was well. At the end of the shift they brought me into the office to speak with a manager. They had their security supervisor present which told me it was bad news and the manager was scared of me and how I might react.

He told me we needed to talk about the previous evening. I thought they were firing me. He said they would suspend me, no shifts for two weeks and next time I touched a client I would be fired. I told them to use those two weeks as my two week notice that I was respectfully tapping out.

"This is bullshit, you used me for this rap concert because you know I will take care of business even though you want to suspend me for barely touching some dick head who needed to be removed." I didn't take this job to get fired or have the owner throw me under the bus, feeling that guy would call the cops on me and be yelled at like a kid. They didn't appreciate my perspective at all.

You got to understand that you are expendable. You need to know yourself, your limits, what you are willing to take, understand your potential hot buttons, pitfalls and personal limitations. I will go hands on when I deem necessary as I am not waiting to get sucker-punched or stabbed in the back before I react to a threat.

The writing was on the wall and I was feeling it was time to move on. The owner says "I don't appreciate your tactics." So, I'm out. They fire me. With reflection, I come to realize that they were in fact wrong…but being right doesn't always turn out "right."

I also realized that it was partly my fault for not knowing about their "no hands on" policy. Also, I should have known that I was working for people that didn't have my back.

"I take the invasion of my personal space very seriously."

Kid Rock

CREATING AND USING THE PHYSICAL ENVIRONMENT

Dave: Creating and using the physical environment; what does that mean to you right from the start?

Gabe: Knowing where walls and other natural obstacles are is important, it helps you strategize your movements and funnel people to certain places. Being able to use tables, chairs and other things that show up in real time that can be used for defense is critical. For instance, if someone pulled a knife, I would want to use a chair to help get distance, keep myself, my team and patrons safe. Then I would smash him if he didn't put it down.

Dave: Is there an area where you would rather have the conflict be if inside the club/ bar based on how things are set up?

Gabe: Yes, I mean no place is a good place to have a violent confrontation but of course some are better than others. For example, I would rather get a violent patron to the front door as soon as possible rather than take him down in the middle of a crowded dance floor. You have to assume there are always friends ready to jump in or sucker punch you at any moment.

I once had to try and get a guy to walk down a metal flight of stairs within a nightclub. Getting him down the stairs without getting physical was the goal. I had no choice but to have my back to a group of his friends as he was cooperating at first. Then he turned and tried to swing on me and luckily I had a team member in front of him on the staircase with me. I blocked the punch and pinned him against the railing. We picked the guy up and tried to carry him down the stairs but he fought us immediately as we tried to gain control of him.

My biggest fear was getting tossed over the railing as we were still a good ways up and he had a group of his friends following behind us. The guy was all coked up and putting up one hell of fight. Somehow I was able to maintain my balance as we eventually got him to the bottom platform and here is where my team members failed me.

Unfortunately you don't know if someone has really got your back until you need it and then, of course, if they don't it's too late. So I think it's fair to say that we were all pretty winded by the time we got to the bottom of the stairs banged up and all.

I remember tossing the guy down the last couple of steps and assumed the security team members at the bottom would finish it up. I walked past him trying to catch my breath figuring my work was done but as I looked up this guy had got to his feet and was heading my way. I defensively stomped kicked him right in his stomach and he flew backwards, stumbled to the floor and got knocked out when his head hit the wall.

Then we had the task of kicking out his entire crew who were now extremely upset with me. This is another reason why I like to stay on top of my cardio because you just never know how long you're going to be going at it.

Dave: The DJ booth is usually above the dance floor at least a step or two. Is this an advantage point for a bouncer to set up to watch over the patrons?

Gabe: It is and has actually served as a "penalty box" if you will for me in the past! [he says laughing]

There have been times when I had an excessive force case pending and we thought it would be better for business if I stayed out of the public's eye since the **perception was** that I had been overly aggressive the night before. What all the witnesses failed to see was that the patron had grabbed my throat and attempted to choke me before I tried to detain him and escort him out.

So I stayed out of the public's eye and from the DJ booth just watched the crowd calling shots from my radio. My instructions from my boss were to only come out of the DJ booth if my team got in over their head and needed my back up.

Dave: How do you strategically use the environment to get to conflicts quickly?

Gabe: That's a good question and one that is so important to look at seriously. With a crowd it can be hard to have a clear path to get to an incident quickly. The last club I work at I was usually posted up a few feet (three steps) above the main bar and dance floor in the VIP section, as I have previously mentioned. Sometimes I hop the railing to get to the dance floor or bar fast if I see a something needing my immediate attention. I usually try to position myself at the top step and keep the steps clear of people so there is nobody in my way if I need to move fast.

Also, if you work in a place where there are chairs or tables you need to be very conscious of not only of what is in front of you but what is behind you and how they can be used for advantage, as well.

Dave: Is there a way to use the environment to get fighting or trouble patrons out of the venue fast?

Gabe: Usually the best way is to get them out the closest exit and sometimes that means bringing them through the kitchen. This can be dangerous too as there are knives and heavy metal pots and pans, glasses etc., that can be used as weapons against you should you lose control of the patron.

Another way is to have the DJ turn the lights on and stop the music calling security to the floor or wherever the trouble spot may be. This helps to get everyone's attention. It's hard for people to get out of your way if they don't see you coming or know what's going on.

Dave: What if the club is packed wall-to-wall with people? How do you get through the crowd to a trouble spot or even get troublemakers out when it's so crowded?

Gabe: This is a tough one and there really isn't anything you can do other then be as polite and as fast as possible. Sometimes it means physically moving people out of your way. A good tactic is to use your flashlight to indicate you're coming through but let's be honest not everyone is facing you. So it's a challenge and you do the best you can. Most people understand what you're dealing with to do your job and actually appreciate your effort, even if it comes across a bit abrasive or rude at first. People know in the long run you are looking out for their overall safety.

It helps to have a team member lead the way through the crowd if you have someone physically wrapped up and are in the process of making them leave. That's the most professional way to do it.

Dave: Can the lights in the club be used as a way to establish a strong security presence?

Gabe: Yes. Like I had mentioned sometimes turning the house lights up is a good indication that there is some type of emergency. Also the fluorescent lights can be used to highlight the presence of security.

Dave: Could you explain more about that?

Gabe: At one venue our uniform shirts had white reflective lettering and the logo was reflective in fluorescent lighting too. So part of the roamer's job was to weave his way in and out of the crowded dance floor in between as many parties as possible, turning and twisting his body around every so often. This would allow a great number of people within the club to see the reflective security writing and logo which gave the appearance that there was a heavy security presence. When in fact it was only one or two people moving around in and out of different crowds every few minutes. A great psychological ploy.

Dave: Very interesting. In the same respect how about the deafening music?

Gabe: Of course the loud music makes it difficult to hear someone speaking right in front of you. The music can certainly be a problem but at times can be used to your advantage in certain situations.

One example is you make the point it's so loud you can't hear so it's a good excuse to get the patron outside to talk. This gets them peacefully removed, usually on their own accord.

A dirty trick that I was taught to use if I think the use of force is inevitable and you want to justify getting the jump on them is move your lips as if your saying something. Actually you are not saying anything at all. They most likely will lean into you in order to hear what you said and when they do aggressively, that's your green light to "defend yourself." This needs to be used as a last resort option, for sure.

Dave: Couches, chairs, railings, stairs; how can these obstacles become beneficial to security personnel?

Gabe: It's all a matter of perspective. We like our paths to be clear when having to physically remove someone. But I have used various objects to my advantage to trap people into a certain space or as leverage points when physically grappling with people. Sometimes people don't realize what's behind them and I've been able to knock people off balance by using objects as stumbling blocks…just keep in mind that it works both ways. You must be aware of your surroundings at all times.

Dave: What about having a shot caller that observes from a high point in the club? How does this work and how is this an asset to the club?

Gabe: After getting my eye socket fractured and having surgery the doctor advised against getting hit again anytime soon…but I didn't want to miss work. So I posted up in the DJ booth which was on the second level of this nightclub but also overlooked the first floor too. It was a great "perch" so to speak where I could see everything. This worked out great as I could call into my team members from the lookout and tell people who and where they needed to go. Worst case scenario I could go help out if need be too.

Also, like in Las Vegas, they call the cameras the "eye in the sky" with people watching everything all the time. I also had a good friend who had a bar in a rough neighborhood. We had video cameras from the bar and throughout restaurant with TV monitor in the back office. We always had a couple of guys in the office watching everything so we could always go out back and come around front to catch any robbers or do whatever needed to be done.

Dave: How important is it to have tables and the bar bussed as soon as possible?

Gabe: Any object can be used as a weapon against you so the getting bottles and glasses off the table as soon as possible is important. Anytime there is broken glass on the floor the risk of injury increases and so getting things cleaned up, spills dried up, all makes for a safer work environment for everyone. Wet, slick floors can be very dangerous too.

REALITY: Making Friends and Enemies

You know you're going to make enemies if you do this job. It's unavoidable. Expect it and it won't impact you the same way.

One venue I worked over twenty years ago was on a rough drug infested avenue in the heart of a city. I used to live just a few blocks from the bar and would walk to work. Well, of course, that means walking home too.

This was before I got sober and I had a couple drinks that night at the end of my shift. I was walking home and stopped at a 7-11 to get something. This particular street was known for gang and drug activity. Kicking an unruly patron out in this neck of the woods could result in a shooting. It wasn't uncommon.

This was a small neighborhood bar and we didn't have too many problems but there was a lot of random street traffic. People who weren't regulars would come and go. Sometimes you'd kick someone out and it resulted in a scuffle outside the club. There were times when people were way out of line and we used to enforce street justice in the alley. Certain bosses never want you to call the cops if possible and even pay you a little extra for handling problems "in house."

Well there's an old saying that what comes around goes around...
So when I finished buying whatever it was I was buying and as I'm leaving the counter, I look up and see this guy walking in as I'm walking out. I recognize him immediately but apparently he doesn't recognize me. I walk out and notice the vehicle that I'm sure is his because the driver seat is empty and I notice another guy I recognize in the passenger seat.

We make eye contact but it's brief. It's just for a second but long enough where my gut tells me he recognized me too and I best start running as soon as I hit the corner of the building! I break into a sprint as fast as I can and within seconds I hear tires screeching. I don't turn to look back but I hear "Hey motherf--ker!" and an engine revving, motor vehicle hauling ass behind me. I veer right across the street noticing their truck speeding towards me. There's nowhere to hide but I run towards houses across the street. "Pop!" "Pop!"

Two gunshots ring out and pierce the night air. I hop over a wooden fence into the back yard of someone's house. It's like 3 in the morning. I blast through the back gate, winded, which leads out into a dark alley. Panting trying to catch my breath, walking hunched over thinking I'll puke any second I hear their truck and see the headlights turning down into the alley. By the time it takes for me to notice them I'm convinced they noticed me as they come charging down the alley.

I scramble looking for a yard to cut through and notice a pathway around a back alley garage that leads into another piece of private property. Running for my life I sprint across this small back lot, hear the truck approaching the entrance I entered and notice a tall iron fence in front of me.

Confident I can scale myself up and over it I leap up and grab the top pointed nubs of the fence to pull myself up. I get one leg up on top in between the fencing and my foot on top of the upper railing. I'm right by the corner of the house which the fence dives into and yank myself up to the top then use the actual house for stability to get my other foot up and stand so I can jump down but as I begin to do so my left foot slips off the railing.

I lose my balance falling down towards the front side of the yard that I was trying to get to but my right upper thigh catches on one of the sharp pointed railing tops as I topple over the fence. It stabs sharply into my upper inside thigh just missing my groin! It must have rained lightly that night as the top of the fence was wet and slick or maybe their sprinklers had been on earlier.

I found myself literally hanging upside down impaled on this fence by my thigh. The adrenaline masked the pain I'm sure because I don't remember feeling a thing. All I could think about was getting myself off this fence before I got shot. I felt like a sitting duck or hanging duck!

After the initial shock wore off that I was a human shish kabob hanging upside down by my thigh I pulled myself up the railings and had enough abdominal strength to assist in curling my body upwards along with my arms to get high enough to free my leg from the iron rail wound. Not sure how I fell without breaking my neck but I remember landing hard.

Scared I would be shot at any moment, either by the scumbags that I had kicked out and fought a few weeks back at the bar or the homeowner, I knew I had to get up and keep moving. At this point I don't remember hearing the vehicle and not sure where these guys were.

Did they park and were on foot hunting me down or did they go to the end of the alley and were about to head down this street I was now facing. I lost all audio clarity it seems when I got impaled on the fence, not sure how, but it really impacted my body and decision making. The night stood still and fell silent and I remember feeling extremely vulnerable for what seemed like a long time but only lasted a second or two. It's possible I was in shock and disbelief at what had just happened to me.

I'm sure I was bleeding but wasn't concerned with stopping the loss of blood. I knew I had to move quickly if I wanted to survive not knowing where my enemy was lurking. I crossed the street, cut through another yard and found an open garage. Finding some type of objects to hide behind I laid down and listened intently for any movement outside.

After several minutes I had finally caught my breath and the pain set in. I was bleeding like a stuck pig, my pant leg soaked with blood. I pulled my t-shirt off and ripped it so I would have double the length to make a good tourniquet to stop the bleeding but the wound was high up my inner thigh. At this point I decided the safest thing to do was get myself back to the main avenue and flag a cop down. I needed medical attention and didn't want to get caught off guard again by these fools if I tried to ninja my way home. Plus with one blood soaked pant leg, no shirt on and a tourniquet I kind of stood out.

The downside of going to the cops was I had a warrant out for my arrest at the time for a parole violation. I was working at the bar under the table, for cash, and working there was a violation of my parole as well as being out past curfew and drinking too.

I figured God spared my life yet again and maybe this was his way of getting my attention to get myself off the streets again and lead a healthy life. This was a period of my life when going to jail and prison was pretty routine. Guess it was time to turn myself in. I got myself back out on the busy avenue where sites like me weren't too uncommon and flagged a patrol car down. They got me an ambulance, handcuffed me to the gurney and I was on my way back into the Big House for a couple years. So glad this is a faded memory of where I am today.

"We were all born with a certain degree of power. The key to success is discovering this innate power and using it daily to deal with whatever challenges come our way."

Les Brown

WORKING THE DOOR, CREATING THE ENERGETIC AND KEEPING THE PEACE

Dave: **How important is the role of the doorman?**

Gabe: The doorman has a tremendously important job. Being the first employee of the establishment the public will meet means that the doorman must make a great first impression. So, great customer service skills are vital but at the same time he must be an expert at making sure he can verify people's identification.

The liquor license of the establishment hinges on the doorman doing a proper job. This is the most important task first and foremost. Screening for over intoxicated incoming patrons is important too. Then of course they screen for dress code and help direct VIP clients to the manager or hostess if the establishment has one.

Dave: What are the most important attributes of a good doorman?

Gabe: Well-groomed appearance, excellent manners, and great people skills. The "gift of gab" helps too! As I have said before, this person really sets the tone of the entire club and ensures that people enter in the right frame of mind. It's like a landlord, it's better to screen as opposed to having to kick someone out later. I expect my doorman to be cordial and carry themselves in a professional manner at all times. Checking every single person's ID as they come through the door and to ensure that anybody asked to leave the establishment does not reenter that evening.

Dave: How can one best prepare to be a doorman? Is there study material for this?

Gabe: The best training for a doorman is to work a few shifts shadowing a well experienced one. Watching how a professional doorman deals with the public is important. Hands on training is really where it's at because no amount of reading is going to provide the detail, body language and pre-fight indicators.

Dave: How many feet is the door man responsible for in front of the bar?

Gabe: It all depends on the city and the specific venue. This is an important fact that security teams must be aware of because if a fight breaks out you are responsible for so many feet maybe outside the club but at a certain point you're not.

This is where you could really get yourself into trouble on a personal level. If you're not covered by the insurance of your security company or your employer, if it's the venue itself, then you could be looking at both criminal and civil action against you. What is considered private property and what is public is an important distinction. You would not want to violate someone's rights and you want to find out these distances before working a single shift.

Dave: How does the doorman regulate a large crowd of people trying to enter the club at the same time?

Gabe: With extreme diligence! You must be as polite and diplomatic as possible but yet stern. You let the people know that it is your goal to get everyone in but it must be done in an orderly fashion. Sometimes if the place is at capacity you must wait for people to leave in order to let people in to the club.

Then, it is important to explain to them that it is a fire code issue and the law. Sometimes management just wants to regulate the flow of the crowd so the rationale for why we do it really depends. It's usually up to the security team to dictate the pace and order of the crowd. A good security team can make this happen. It is important not just for the appearance outside the club to look professional and safe but for genuine safety itself. You don't want people getting trampled or hurt in any capacity.

Dave: How does the doorman regulate the crowd after hours when the club is closed or when he wants people away from the front of the venue?

Gabe: Way too often people want to mingle outside the club after hours when you've shut down. Its trouble you don't need and the sooner you can get everyone off the private property the better.

A tactic we would use at one venue was to get a leaf blower out as if we were using it to clean up out front. The noise from the machine makes it so people can't have a conversation so they usually move elsewhere.

Dave: Why would a doorman use a counter to keep track of people entering and exiting the establishment?

Gabe: Counters are real helpful to keep from allowing too many people into a venue and finding yourself in violation of the law. A good doorman would keep accurate count of all people coming and going. This is an excellent way to stay on top of this issue. This is why organization and attention to detail can be important. To some it might sound like a silly question, but if you don't measure, you won't know. So, if you want to ensure you are not in violation, don't rely on the doorman keeping track of it in his head.

Dave: What if the doorman discovered someone using fake ID?

Gabe: It's the law that if you discover a fake ID that you must confiscate it and give it to the police. A good tactic is to tell a suspected underage person about the law and how you strictly enforce it…that you have zero tolerance of people trying to get over on you. Then after a good serious no nonsense stare I ask them if they still want to show their ID or do they think it would be better to leave and never attempt this again at your club? The best bet is to check with local law enforcement on the exact law and procedure they expect you to follow and then do so.

Dave: What are your thoughts on equipment that you think bouncers should and should not use to help keep the peace?

Gabe: I think they should us any type of force multiplier (weapons) that are legal. I think better safe than sorry. With that, how to use, retain and when appropriate to go to those weapons is critical. No brass knuckles or illegal weapons. But I think people need to consider whether you want at least one person trained with a gun…look at the active shooter issues happening now. One highly skilled person with a gun is a game changer. Maybe that's not popular to say, but that's reality. I like that quote you have Dave, "Are you preparing for the ideal world you want or the real world we have?"

Dave: Do you think it is important to have security briefings; and, if so, what would they look and sound like?

Gabe: Yes, absolutely. We have mentioned this in some ways throughout; a checklist is really good and a meeting that covers current issues, who are consistent trouble makers, escalation of force issues and more. After shift meetings are almost more important sometimes, but both should be used. Looking back and reflecting on everything that happened makes for a more cohesive team and smoother run establishment. Maybe it doesn't have to be that formal, but something needs to be done before and after the shift. Owners and team members are counting on each other to protect one another and everyone's best interest.

Dave: What is your experience with the value of having procedures and policies around searching patrons?

Gabe: Let's go right to the issues of active shooters at multiple clubs…this goes beyond basics ideology. Before we worried about people smuggling booze, now it's weapons. You need a well-regulated door with everyone waiting and watching while real searches happen; doing this before anyone comes in is critical. And patrons should see that you are doing this for two reasons: 1) it makes them feel safer; and 2) anyone who thought about trying to bring a weapon in will see that he will get caught and the police will be called. All other exits have to be watch and checked. Also, check employee lockers; are they brining weapons into the club themselves? It should be like the airport really.

Dave: Any particular strategies on having masses of people get in line and keeping people peaceful?

Gabe: No, I just look at them and look mean. You really have to be an ass, because they don't respect anything…most are drinking, some smart ass will always try to tell you "where to go" and then when it's his time to go in after waiting, you just say no.

REALITY: Check Yourself!

There's a learning curve when you're a professional bouncer and you either get better at your job or you burn your own bridge. I used to take things so personal and get so mad when people were in my face, running their mouths, whining, "Why are you kicking my friend out?" or "you're not a cop, you can't do nothing to me." Whether it's with a confrontational tone or an act of physical aggression it all increases the levels at an already stressful job... that can get much more stressful.

"I don't have to explain anything," used to be my attitude but you're not in the thug business, you're in a customer service position as you're representing the owner and the establishment itself. But no matter how cordial or diplomatic you try to be with some of the patrons in a club they just don't get it or don't care and the other thing you got to remember is that just about all of them are wasted!

It was so hard for me in the beginning to walk away or let the verbal abuse roll off my shoulders. I found it so incredibly hard not to get sucked into somebody else's problem because I was so wrapped up in my own social defects that everything was personal to me. An ego struggle can happen at any moment. When this happens it is a sure sign of lacking professionalism; we can't play by our own rules and see everything as a personal challenge instead of an opportunity to test and increase my professional skill set.

Eventually I was blessed with the opportunity to work with some solid professionals that taught me many tricks of the trade. Like when you feel yourself getting agitated and taking things personal to "hand off the incident'" to another security team member. This is a great lesson learned that I suggest people use. That's the responsible thing to do but it comes with knowing yourself and being mature enough to take the high road…and as you say Dave, streamlining our ego.

If you are going to take a job where people are going to be intoxicated you need to expect some of those people to get mouthy, they will not comprehend reason or what you're saying because they are drunk. Putting yourself in an environment where management's goal is to sell as much booze as possible and not to expect chaos is a pipedream. If you have this mentality, you are in the wrong business. Your job is to be as kind and accommodating as possible while upholding the integrity and security of the establishment and its clientele.

Don't let this job become an outlet for your insecurities or a place for you to throw tantrums when your unrealistic expectations are not met. You better check yourself before you get checked.

"NBC had a show called 'The Toughest Bouncer in America' that I did. But I told them I didn't like that term, 'bouncer.' To me, it's offensive. A bouncer likes to get physical, likes to put his hands on people."

Mr. T

CONTROLLING PHYSIOLOGY AND OUR VERBAL AND NONVERBAL BODY LANGUAGE

Dave: Tell me how important it is to know how your psychological and physiological chemical reactions will affect your response in high-stress situations?

Gabe: Man, it's so important. If you can't handle the cascade of chemical changes that will happen when you get hit with that adrenaline dump you could really hurt somebody, get hurt or worse. You must first be a master of your domain before you can even consider trying to control someone else in a safe manner.

If you freeze up over react because you're not used to responding under stress you could open yourself up for both criminal and civil liability. Not to mention hurting or killing someone.

Another thing is you must be able to make decisions in a heartbeat about whether force is needed or not. You must be in control of your emotions and psychologically sound to be a professional in this business. Your life and freedom and those of others are on the line. All it takes is one bad night, one bad decision and life as you know it will change.

Dave: How does one train for this?

Gabe: Stress induced drills; my choices of course are my Krav Maga classes and training events. You need to get your heart rate up above 140 beats a minute because the increased heart rate mimics the physiological symptoms of stress.

Also role playing and scenario reality based drills (which we have mentioned) are most effective to help with the proper mindset. You must know what the adrenaline dump feels like so you can recognize the symptoms when they happen to you. The more familiar one is of being in that physiological and emotional state the easier it becomes to navigate through it when duty calls.

I think some basic psychology training to help people identify their own personal triggers and how to work through them is also important. If a person is real insecure they will take verbal abuse personally and unfortunately it comes with the job. Intoxicated people get "mouthy" and you've got to let it roll off of you. People will sometimes purposely push your buttons to see how far they can push you or to bait you to hit them first. You must be able to read people and see through the games they're playing, recognize their motives or strategy and use your words if you can.

Dave: Do you want your physical presence to be intimidating?

Gabe: It definitely can help for sure. Having a big guy at the door is usually a good idea but not always necessary. The size of an individual can deter some from getting out of line because they may fear the consequences. So, it can be a huge psychological benefit.

Being in good shape helps as well but I've seen that it doesn't matter how big or strong you appear when the time comes to get physical. What matters is whether or not you have the skills to use your size and strength in the capacity needed to get the job done.

I'm only 5'9 and usually weigh between 200-215lb, not necessarily the biggest guy so I depend more on my facial expression to communicate my confidence. How I carry myself and my body language is my first line of defense and offense!

I want people to know just by looking at me that I am all business and confident that I will handle whatever is put in my path that needs handling.

The best offense is a strong defense. The best defense includes preventive measures. I try to kill them with kindness and give them every opportunity to walk in peace. How you carry yourself speaks volumes, this can be taught and it's a discipline.

Dave: What can you communicate with your facial expressions and posturing alone?

Gabe: I have a couple of "poses" that are meant to communicate a couple different things. One is to act uninterested or bored and another is my standard "club stance."

My face can sometimes have a smile on it but for the most part I like to look serious. In a club where people are having fun and socializing I like to be that one anchor point of seriousness that stands out in the midst of the party. I will become a reference point for a guy whose eyes are constantly scanning the club and taking direct notice of those taking notice of him. I let them know I see them eye balling me.

Dave: Why is this important?

Gabe: I feel it's important because looking down or away is a sign of weakness or intimidation. I let them know that I've done this a million times before and I signed up do it again tonight. It's a form of psychological warfare, really. I don't try to stare anyone down but I let them know I see them and move on since my responsibility is to watch the entire club, not just them. You're letting them know that they are not that significant in my world, a dime a dozen and that you know exactly where they are in the crowd. I can let them know that just by looking at them.

Another technique I use is that I may even make pretend I am talking into my microphone about them when in fact it's just an act. It is a way for me to let them think we are watching them and have reason to be suspicious of them. This of course is only for those I suspect are looking for trouble. You want them know to know that it's not a good idea without having to say anything.

Dave: How can you use people's natural body language to your advantage?

Gabe: People clenching the hands or teeth are pretty obvious signs before an aggressor fully initiates a violent outburst. Other signs ranging from faster paced breathing to something as subtle as pupillary constriction can be signs that you may want to prepare yourself for oncoming violence or take the initiative and launch a pre-emptive strike to ensure your personal safety.

Dave: How do you best control your composure when confronting a potential violent situation?

Gabe: I use self-talk within my head to calm my nerves and help me keep things in perspective while relying on practiced breathing exercises. Deep breaths in thru the nostrils and hold...then exhale slowly through the mouth. I do my best to stay conscious of my breathing and actively listen to my self-talk and to get more oxygen to the brain.

You want to base your decisions on facts outside the scope of how you feel about something emotionally. You must question your own motives for wanting to take certain actions, especially if you are capable of causing serious bodily harm.

Dave: Are there advantages that you can utilize to best harness these cascade of chemicals as they are released into your system?

Gabe: I think so. I personally know how to harness my adrenaline and combine that with visualization. I see myself taking the necessary action before I unleash myself. I see it in real time and follow it all the way through in my mind because everything has slowed down…that's the benefit of training and repetition.

Usually I will try to use my words and keep myself under leash as the scenario plays out over and over again in my head as I am talking or listening as I am watching their hands and scanning my surroundings. My exit path is also chosen, my tactics waiting in the wings of my mind.

Some people have no idea how close they came to getting themselves hurt and I know this may sound like I am overly aggressive but you must understand that my goal each shift is to go home safe. I always give the other guy the benefit of the doubt. Assuming he is stronger, faster and highly skilled fighter. I prepare for the worst so I can deliver my best professional reaction if necessary.

I tell myself, " WE DON"T LOSE" and "WE DON'T QUIT," then I go.

Dave: Tell me some of your best nonverbal secrets and why they work?

Gabe: My best nonverbal secret are my hands up in front of my face, sometimes in "praying" like position and transitioning back and forth to palms out with open hands facing opponent. From here I can easily block or strike or both simultaneously with the ability to deliver a decisive blow to the eyes, ears, throat, nose.

The goal is to totally disrupt their thought process while either gaining control of them, causing damage or both. Although, as mentioned many times, non-violent techniques are preferred. That said, sometimes it is not possible.

The best nonverbal secret is a surprise attack. We use deception in our posturing, words and how we approach the situation. Sometimes a good hard stare can get your point across but with poor lighting it's sometimes best to act uninterested and bored so you don't come across as an immediate threat. This approach usually has them subconsciously lower their guard.

REALITY: The OODA Loop

Training specifically for bouncing as a martial artist is quite different then training for sport or competition. We beat our opponents first and foremost psychologically and physiologically. Having a general understanding of these two key components and knowing how to leverage them to our advantage is the key to success in this business. I learned this from my Krav Maga training.

Studying the OODA loop which is a model developed by Colonel John Boyd on how we make decisions when facing violence gives anyone the upper hand in combat. Basically it's an acronym for Observe, Orient, Decide and Act. Learning not to freeze up when attacked or how to make other people freeze up if you need to go hands on is what you want to master. This can only come through proper training.

Let's say you get sucker punched. That is an action by the bad guy. You **OBSERVE** the fact that something hit you or observe the pain you feel from being hit. Then you **ORIENT** to the situation, try to get your bearings in reference to what you just perceived. Next you must **DECIDE** what to do or how to react, then of course you **ACT**. Rinse, cycle, repeat.

Now we have been struck. If you know this is how the human mind works then you can use different tactics to your advantage. For example Retzef is a Hebrew word for "continuous" and in reference to Krav Maga (Contact Combat in Hebrew) Retzef means "continuous motion" or "continuous pressure." So unlike traditional sparring like we see in most martial arts we train in Retzef which is more of a flow type drill of a flurry, if you will, of strikes. Usually high followed by low striking to the opponents body.

In traditional sparring you dance around and wait for an opening to strike, you exchange blows with your opponent. You see by doing this your giving your opponent time to recalibrate: **observe, orient, decide, act** and vice versa but in our world we don't want to give the bad guy an opportunity to act. To do this most effectively we must disrupt his thought process.

We need to overwhelm them with something to keep them from efficiently reacting to what we want to deliver. This is done by distracting their mind and keeping them in the OODA loop. Their mind is like the reset button on a computer. We need to overwhelm it with information so they stay preoccupied with trying to sort it out in order to prevent them from formulating a plan and fighting back.

This doesn't have to be done using only physical distractions like launching projectiles with our hands, elbows, feet, knees and head or causing damage using them or a weapon with precision ballistic striking. You can also use your words to disrupt their thought process, you can yell, scream, give direction and more. The goal is to get them actively listening or talking, this keeps them from formulating a plan for a second or two which is enough time for you to act.

For example a guy comes up and is yelling in my face after we have to escort his drunk girlfriend out of the club because she fell over and spilled her drink on another girl which just about started a fight. He's screaming at me, I can see the veins popping out of his neck. I'm watching his hands out of my peripheral vision. He balls up his first. Engaging him in conversation, often trivial questions, just to keep his mind busy is a good tactic to keep him from thinking his way out of the OODA loop as we physically advance on him. By the time he observes and orients to what I'm doing, I am already acting. The goal is to be three steps ahead of him and in an advantageous position before he even decides on how he will act. It's really a beautiful thing once you fully understand it and see it unfold before you.

If this does not work, I launch preemptively by popping his right shoulder with a palm strike as I simultaneously reach behind and hook his left shoulder violently pulling it in towards me. It's a "push pull" motion that flips him around as I move to get up behind him and with my right thumb side of my first now on his jaw bone I press it in tightly by cupping my left hand around my right fist. This is called a face lock. Yet, there is always something to think about next.

As I do this to escort the on guy out, one of his friends reacts and starts to move toward me. I yank the guys face back and down as I pop his knee out from behind and drop him. His friend who is moving towards me, fists clenched in a fighting stance is several feet away from me. With my hands up in a ready fighting position my training kicks in. I realize and observe that I must close the distance. I perceive that the guy is a threat and I decide to overwhelm him with distraction strikes that may or may not cause damage but by launching them from long range disrupts his thought pattern long enough for me to get into medium range.

I kick his groin but barely make contact. It's enough to get him to flinch. I close the distance by throwing a jab to his face but his hands are up and it lands on his fists (but again it's enough to disrupt his thoughts of attacking me because he is reacting to the jab). This buys me another half second to pull both his arms down just far enough to release them and spring in to him at close range to "bear hug" his head and get "surgical."

Once I trap his head I have the command center which makes all the decisions for the rest of his body. Then depending on the threat level I can either take him down to detain him or deliver strategic ballistic shots that cause damage like a head butt or elbow to his face.

In most cases there's no need to cause serious damage but, if I need to, I can smash his nose with a palm strike while spinning him around from the opposite shoulder just like the "push/pull" motion of the face lock…but this time one hand pulls his left shoulder in as my other hand blows out his sinus cavity as it compress his nose into his face. Then, as I spin him around facing away from me my hands move to cover both his eyes and depending on his size and strength I can either drill my knee into his back or pop out his knee with my foot from behind as I crank his head back and down which puts a tremendous amount of stress on the brain stem.

Then I simply sit him down in front of me and transition him into a cuffing position or apply some type of arm bar or wrist lock. Sometimes if I see him going for a weapon, I just continue to get surgical on his head until I can control him properly.

"The supreme art of war is to subdue the enemy without fighting."

Sun Tzu

9

HANDS-ON TECHNIQUES AND SEPARATING FIGHTING PATRONS

Dave: What are the most hands on techniques that you have for escorting patrons out of the bar?

Gabe: Here is the quick list:

- Arm Bar
- Goose Neck
- Wrist Lock
- Chicken Wing
- Face Lock
- Finger Lock
- Four Guys…one on each limb

Dave: What are the best technical skills to have for when someone throws a wild haymaker punch?

Gabe: 360 Defense from Krav Maga, blocking and striking at the same time. Then I will wrap him up. You could also duck and do a double leg take down, however ideally you don't want to be in a ground fight.

Dave: What are the basic rules you operate by with respect to distance?

Gabe: Stay at least three feet away, arm's length and maybe two. A basic ready stance…we ask, we tell, we make.

Dave: Are there certain techniques that you know and want to use but can't?

Gabe: That's funny Dave. Carotid choke would be the first thing that comes to mind. It is very risky, same with any strike to the neck…it would have to be a lethal situation.

Dave: How do you best handle two patrons in the midst of fighting each other?

Gabe: It's all situational because there are so many different factors that come into play here. The number one thing is you need to separate those fighting as soon as possible.

Let's take a general one-on-one situation as our baseline. In a perfect world you have back up right there and you each are able to handle one guy. You stop the fight usually with some type of arm bar or wrist lock and exit the two out of different exits. Maybe one guy goes out the back and one goes out the front.

Dave: Is there a certain protocol of procedures?

Gabe: You never want to go in alone. Always call on the radio that there is a fight and where it is happening. Then, you wait for back up. If the guys are killing each other and you're by yourself, call the police. But otherwise you want to get the aggressor off of whoever is getting beaten.

Going in alone is a bad idea because every offender usually has a couple of jerk friends hanging out with him who will jump to his aide if you intervene. What truly sucks is usually you don't know who started it, not that it matters, but a guy might be defending himself. Either case, you do your best to end it before someone gets hurt. Your personal safety comes first…just like the oxygen mask on the airplane scenario.

Dave: What if someone argued that it might be best to sometimes stand back and call the police?

Gabe: All depends, if you see a guy getting his face smashed into the floor and you can restrain the guy on top from causing serious bodily harm then you do so immediately. You probably can't wait for the police to respond since someone is getting hurt and you are responsible for keeping the customers safe. Again it's all situational, depends on if you have back up team members there, your skill set and the risks involved. The police should be called regardless if someone assaults anyone.

Dave: What if it's outside the club? What is the protocol for breaking up fights when it's outside on the public sidewalk in front of the club?

Gabe: If it's not on private property or outside what the city deems is the club's responsibility then it's not your problem. Getting involved could open you up to all sorts of legal problems, so then it comes down to your own morals, values and belief system whether you want to get involved or not.

Dave: What if there are more than just two people fighting? Does a single bouncer get involved?

Gabe: A single bouncer should never get involved in something he may not be able to handle. This is why communication on the radio needs to be clear and concise. It is critical. I do my best to keep a visual on each one of my security team members as well.

Dave: How do you know how much force to use?

Gabe: Well this comes with experience. So guys may be so scared of hurting someone they don't use enough force or they are complacent or over confident with their skills and it backfires on them.

On the flip side if you use too much then you are open to legal problems and the psychological effects of trauma that may arise from hurting someone else. You must be tough skinned and be able to choose wisely in the heat of the moment. It's a very fine line between doing your job properly and keeping yourself safe.

Dave: Are you introducing "Force Multipliers" to help control or get control of an out-of-control situation?

Gabe: I have worked nightclub security in a city where all my guys on the door were armed with guns. I even worked an armed security post at a Reggae Bar that was located in more of an industrial part of town where the police had very poor response time. This place had had 5 shootings in their parking lot and bar in the first two months they were open.

It was gang related activity. I personally am unable to legally carry a firearm but I know how to use one, did some tactical and executive protection (3rd party) shooting training. I worked with a very well trained soldier as he was a former Navy special ops guy. He backed his car by the front door with a couple of assault rifles in the trunk. We were sent in to regulate. Crazy.

That location we "wanded" (hand held metal detector) everyone before entering. But some of the nightclubs I worked for as a supervisor with a certain company we wore Navy blue BDU's, bullet proof vests, carried O.C. spray, Asp baton, Taser, handcuffs, tactical cut off gloves with Kevlar knuckles and I always carried a knife or two.

Dave: Can you give me an example of when non-lethal weapons might be used?

Gabe: A great example is when a guy assaulted one of our doormen outside the club. It turned into more of a wrestling match. I happened to notice it out of the corner of my eye as I was making my rounds inside the club and ran out to help him. There was a second guy trying to jump my team member so I assumed he was gaining control and didn't want the other guy jumping into rescue his buddy…so I took on that guy.

He eventually ran off and the other somehow took off too. My boss was very upset with me because my coworker had his pistol holstered on his hip and that could have been a lethal situation. I was reprimanded for not grabbing the guy wrestling my team member first and using my O.C. spray right into his face and nostrils. I had never trained for a situation like this and assumed my team member could handle it.

In another incident you could use your O.C. spray, outside the club only to break up a fight that was out of control. You were only allowed to spray them if you couldn't physically stop it. Then, when they can't see you can manage them a bit easier. Over spray is a bitch though! That happens often.

Dave: Is there still a chance of you or your staff getting hurt even when all precautions have been taken to keep yourself safe? How do you justify taking such a risk?

Gabe: There's always the risk of injury on the job. This is why becoming highly skilled with using your words to prevent potentially violent situations is so important. Not to mention your self-defense fighting skills and control tactics.

I justify the risk because it is a live arena to practice my art of Krav Maga which first and foremost teaches to avoid dangerous conflict, use words to deescalate a possible violent situation and only use Krav Maga if you must physically protect yourself.

We also use a lot of trapping and various locks from Jujitsu as Krav Maga is a melting pot of the most effective techniques from other systems along with the Israeli ingenuity of what's most practical to keep safe. Obviously many techniques were created for the military to eliminate a threat if necessary and we use modified techniques for the civilian world. Imi Lichtenfeld, the founder of Krav Maga, had a saying that "you should be so good that you don't have to kill."

I learned a lot of good lessons working with so many people on a weekly basis that it became a gold mind to hone my skills and have plenty of information and real life examples to share with my students. For me, I am always a student first so it's like attending a conflict management university (one of your specialties Dave.) Always learning and building new skills/tactics that I can pass on to future generations.

Dave: Live side/dead side – Can you elaborate on that concept for those who don't understand these terms mean and share why you feel it's so important?

Gabe: The "Live Side" is the front of a person's body where they can use their limbs as weapons to strike or kick you. From their shoulder line back is considered their "Dead Side" and this is determined by where they are standing in relation to you…usually to the side of the person where they cannot strike you with their "weapons."

Live side gives your opponent full view of all your weapons (limbs) and optimal striking ability. This is dangerous and most advantageous for your opponent. The dead side of your opponent is a lot safer for you to be on. I have several techniques that get me there quickly and relatively safely. I say relatively because there are no magic techniques. Sometimes you take a punch or two but for the most part when you've got a lot of training and you understand the concepts of time and distance, how to get from point "A" to point "B" and that words of deception help you get a jump on an opponent…things generally run smoothly in your favor.

Once I can get to their dead side I usually try to get directly behind them and use my hands to shut the lights out (placing them over their eyes.) Then I jerk the head back towards me, I may pop their knee or spine forward to knock them off balance with my foot or knee. Then I quickly take a short step back and seat them down in front of me. From here I can strike their face, neck and groin.

It's not always necessary to strike them; it just depends on their level of resistance. Best case scenario is I have team members backing me up and from the seated position my people each grab a limb and carry him out. Depending on his cooperation level usually determines how gently we let him back onto his feet. Sometimes he needs to be detained and handcuffed, other times will let him leave on his own two feet.

Control means control. If he's resisting you do not have control. When you can get to their back then they can't fight back as easily because you are behind them and it will be easier to control them. We usually would try to gain control of the opponent from that position.

REALITY: Time for an Ass Kicking?!

Let's be honest, nobody wants to get their ass kicked. I'd be lying if I said that it does not bother me when I get a call over the radio in a nightclub stating I need to remove a guy from the club and when I get there he's a foot taller and 100lbs heavier. It's happened numerous times and my tactics always follow the same principles.

These huge guys are no different because the guy is large, however there is definitely a bit more apprehension in my approach because the first initial thought upon seeing these giants is, "Shit, this going to hurt." And, while I know my mind shouldn't go there (but I'm just being honest) because I assume the worst and mentally prepare for it.

[That's usually how my self-talk begins in these situations. It's a process and recognizing your fears in the moment is vital to overcoming them. Anyone who says they're scared of nothing is full of shit. Having said that, when I see a bigger man that I may have to man handle I may have a sense of doom but that is really stupid because that means I have a sense of complacency when the patron in question is my size or smaller. This is not good because anyone, any size, can kill you and I teach not to underestimate anyone but I think it's a natural response ingrained in me from my past. So the first thing to do is recognize the facts for what they are, same with your physiological changes.]

I observe my initial thought and feeling, then I tell myself this guy is no different than any other guy, "He's just a man and breaks like any other man." That's the first hurdle and you have to get that out of the way.

Next you tell yourself that we're going to assess the situation and do everything that can be done to solve this problem with words; yet importantly, I'm also choosing targets, watching hands, scanning around me and in front of me and in this case, beyond the giant. (I've had people run up from behind a subject that I was dealing with and try to sucker punch me. You have to expect the unexpected).

My go to with a larger man is his knees. It doesn't always have to be a kick and most times you're in close range so it could be a knee to a knee, knee to the nerve on the inner thigh to displace him and knock him off balance or hard knee shot to the groin. Every action has a reaction and taking away a big guy's balance and stability is the first step for me. From here we can assess if we can get on his arm to apply a wrist lock, gooseneck, arm bar or any other control escort tactic that is applicable.

Of course we don't just hit a guy for no reason but if you feel threatened and you can justify using force then I'm all about it. Not using force, hoping for the best or hesitating with your attack opens you up to getting injured and my goal each night is getting back home uninjured.

Once you strike the knee or the groin it usually gets the subject to buckle over a bit so he actually delivers his head into your hands. From there the option to go to work is never greater and I take full advantage of it because getting tackled by a bigger man in a crowded club with broken glass possibly on the floor doesn't appeal to me.

I always carry knives and have been known to have razor blades stuck in the heels of my boots. I leave the handle of the blade exposed on either side of either boot. I've had my head pounded into the pavement and vowed that'll never happen again. I will cut my way out if I feel trapped. Something most people don't think about when they are raised fighting fair with rules.

My philosophy is that I have a job to do and working in an environment where people are intoxicated…this is not for sport. I'm there to enforce the rules if they are broken and if someone is trying to hurt me I will do whatever it takes not to get hurt. Those are my rules that I adhere to and that's why I train and do as much as I can to handle situations standing. I go to work each night prepared for the fight of my life because you never know what the evening will bring you…I plan on seeing the day that follows.

Luckily by the grace of God I've never had to cut or stab anybody on the job or use any of my other tools for that matter like a Taser, O.C. spray, ASP Baton, and other non-lethal tools. I'm very proficient with my hands and the rest of my body. The real source of strength and ultimate weapon is your mind. Keep it sharp and with luck you'll stay safe.

Yes, I said "luck." Believe what you want but know this: You must do everything in your power to control each situation because there are so many variables that you have to deal with, in your own body and with others. But luck also plays a part.

You train and prepare the best you can to take charge and control the outcomes you need to prevail in this business. The rest is luck and I have trained extremely hard to be the best I could be at my job -- but I'm not naive enough to think I'm some type of super human bouncer. I'm just a man and I've been "lucky." Some call this God's grace or attribute it to the universe; it doesn't matter.

The bottom line is that this is extremely dangerous work. We have to respect the customers as we work for them. Without them there is no work. We are there to help them have fun and be safe, even if they're acting like fools or disrespecting you. Even if they are trying to hurt us, we must remain professional.

Remember, all it takes is one bad night and it's all over. Life in prison is no joke and if you think you're having a bad day just try missing one! Everyday above ground is a good day. Value life. Yours and others. We're all in this together.

"As our enemies have found we can reason like men, so now let us show them we can fight like men also."

Thomas Jefferson

10

AFTER HOURS

Dave: After-hours, parking lots and substance abuse, what's the deal?

Gabe: Parking lots for clubs can be very dangerous, especially patrolling them alone. Vehicles make for 3000lb blunt objects to get hit with and unless armed I wouldn't be out there unless a couple of my team members were by my side carrying and that I knew I could count on them.

Dave: What are the pros and cons of working after hours parties?

Gabe: The pros are I get paid about triple what my hourly rate is in the club and I make a lot of great new contacts. I get to meet a lot of interesting people who I might not normally be in the position to meet. This of course can turn into future employment opportunities.

The cons are you now need workman's comp if you get hurt and if it's a house party and you are also open to so much liability. Plus if you're alone, working it like I was this past winter when we had the X-Games in Aspen, if there's an all-out brawl there's not much you can do about it.

I act more as the sober liaison to keep the police, if they show up, from coming in the house if I can help it, watch that nobody is destroying the property of the homeowner, help the VIP's get privacy when they want it, and mainly make sure everybody leaves when the homeowner wants everybody gone.

This is not an easy task to do by yourself, if you can imagine the situation at 6am after these people have been up partying all day and night. I have a reputation for becoming very aggressive when I feel a justifiable threat, thus the nickname "The Pit Bull," so when several guys gave me a hard time for about an hour after I threatened to call the police and have them arrested, I decided to help them leave.

In this instance I was outnumbered and after the initial attempted assault on me I unleashed The Pit Bull. Nobody really wants a dog that bites until they need one. You still have to make it to your vehicle safely and hope there are no legal ramifications. There is a lot more risk involved freelancing but the reward is usually greater in the end.

Dave: Do you recommend the Moonlighting gigs for your security team?

Gabe: It always helps to have back up but if somebody's got a beef with you then you are real vulnerable outside your work environment. This would depend on the person because if someone is not streetwise, I would say no. They must be realistic about their skill set and experience or it can turn out really bad for them.

Dave: What are some of the risk of security securing a parking lot of bars and nightclubs?

Gabe: People may not be able to bring weapons into the club but a lot of people will have guns in their cars. You can get blindsided in drive by shooting or a hit and run by a vehicle. We had several shootings in one of the cities I worked in where our guys returned fire, someone even pulled an AK-47 out of his trunk one night.

Dave: How can parking lots best be managed?
Gabe: Keeping them well lit, inviting local law enforcement to patrol as often as possible, and patrolling in two's if on foot. Guards should be armed according to local and state laws.

Dave: Can you tell us of an example of the high risks involved with parking lot Security in the nightclub and bar industry?

Gabe: We found a guy sleeping in his car with his firearm in his lap. Like I said above, we have had a couple of shootings and a very unfortunate incident where a young man was shot and killed. I had not been working for that company at that time but it raised tensions very high in that community and then the staff really was on high alert. Lots of stories like that, for sure.

Dave: How do you handle substance abuse among the staff as a security professional?

Gabe: Zero tolerance. They can't get high or drunk on the job. It affects their judgement and when they hurt somebody and have to talk to law enforcement they can be hauled off and drug tested. If the police feel a crime has been committed this will get worse. This can jeopardize the whole business and one bad seed could ruin a company's reputation.

Dave: How about the patrons?
Gabe: Adults can make their own choices, but if we see drug consumption then they have to leave. I usually tell them we called the cops and they can leave now before they arrive. In some cities where I was licensed we were required by law to

detain anyone we witnessed committing a felonious act. Better check with your local law enforcement agency

Dave: What about drug dealers in the bar or club; what is Security's role in keeping people safe while staying within the legal parameters?

Gabe: If we know they are dealing drugs they have to go immediately. Again, you tell them the manager is calling the police and you give them an out. Again, it depends on the club policy and local law enforcement requirements for these specific things.

Dave: How about the substance abuse among non-security staff like bartenders and cocktail waitresses; does security have a role in regulating this and if so what is it?

Gabe: That's up to management if they want me to tell them I am aware of it or not. I've had to escort employees off the property that were overly intoxicated.

Dave: How does substance abuse among owners and managers affect the security professional and what is he to do if he knows about it?

Gabe: I tend to keep my mouth shut if they are paying me well and not mistreating me. If they become verbally abusive they will lose a good employee because I won't stand for that type of behavior. For the most part there's a lot of partying going on and sometimes you wind up babysitting the management or owners to make sure they either make it home safely or you stay all night with them to keep them safe. One hand washes the other. I believe in taking care of the hand that feeds me. Drug culture, regardless of who it is, goes against my life values now. This can be a real downside to the industry and something I definitely do not miss.

Dave: Should Security Professionals be trained in basic Medical Emergency Response procedures in case there's a drug overdose or over intoxication such as alcohol poisoning within the club?

Gabe: I think any medical training is beneficial and should be in the policy of the security company to have some type of medical training and at least a bare minimum of CPR training. Drug education is not a bad idea either. They need to know what to look for and how to handle overdoses and over intoxication of alcohol.

Dave: What happens if there is an all-out brawl?

Gabe: I might just call the cops and not do anything…what am I really going to do?

Reality: VIP

I was working the VIP section in this club and one of the customers was making small talk with me. I usually try not to engage if I can help it as I find it distracting but I always try to be as cordial and polite as possible. Plus you never know what kind of new opportunities might present themselves.

So it turns out that this guy had a small business booking strippers for bachelor parties and wanted to know if I wanted some part time work driving these girls to gigs and making sure they were safe. It paid an hourly rate plus the girls would give you a percent of their tips. I was a single guy back then and it sounded like easy money so I thought, "Why not!"

In fact the guy told me if I wanted he had two girls that had a party to go to after the club closed. The girls were part of his party and if I wanted I could escort them to this guy's house who was there with a bunch of his buddies. These girls were the late night entertainment. He introduced me to the two girls and one of them really caught my eye.

Being young and full of testosterone I liked the idea of playing bodyguard and thought maybe I could hook up with one or both of them by the end of the night. I agreed and as far as I understood the girls were not prostitutes. They were to do a full strip, bottomless, and stay for an hour. They basically would put on an erotic show but that was it. I was supposed to be there just in case any of the men got a little to touchy feely with them.

Well at the end of the night we agreed to leave my old car in the parking lot and I would drive one of their cars since it was a cool little sports car and they had been drinking all night. We get to this house in a pretty nice upper middle class neighborhood and there were a lot of cars parked along the side of this street in front. There must have been 15 to 20 guys there and except for an uncle and the father in law these guys were all hammered.

The two sober fellows showed us to a back bedroom where the girls could get changed and freshen up. The party was downstairs in a finished basement. Well by this time it was pretty apparent that the one stripper I was making eye contact with all night liked me. She had been leaning into me and touching me a bit when I was driving as both girls were in the front with me in the little two seater.

They began undressing in front of me and I respectfully excused myself from the room. I went down stairs to meet the bachelor and his friends. I was supposed to collect the rest of the payment for the girls from them. I assessed the situation and realized that fighting one of these guys would mean fighting all of them as they were all buddies. I had no back up and was in their home. That was my first hint that maybe I shouldn't be there. The bodyguard fantasy with "a piece of a-- as a fringe benefit" got the better of my sound judgement (but I was young and the show was about to begin.)

The girls worked the crowd very well with their seductive bisexual act and before I knew it they were handing me fist fulls of dollar bill tips that they were accumulating. Then they were sitting guys one by one under their crotch and pouring beer between their cleavage allowing it to run down along their bodies and into the guys open mouth.

That's when the first guy asked me how much it was to have sex with one of them. I told him they weren't hookers as far as I knew and I was just there to drive them and get them home safe. Well he didn't like that answer and was getting a little too close for my comfort as he kept on about how much money he'd give me if I could just make it happen.

Then one of the guys snatched one of them up, she's fully naked mind you, and she tries to play along with his "play" but I can tell by her look that she wanted down. So, I politely tell the guy to please put her down. I can see out the corner of my eye the guy who thought I was their pimp mean mugging me and talking to another guy who is staring at me too. The girl that was flirting with me tells me they need a break and want to run upstairs for a few minutes so I shut the music off and make an announcement.

There's mumbling going on and I hear comments like "it hasn't been an hour yet," and I'm getting a really bad feeling. I wasn't packing a gun that night and was feeling pretty vulnerable. I asked the uncle if he could keep these guys downstairs while the girls freshened up, to give them a little privacy for a few minutes. He agreed.

Next thing I know I'm upstairs making out in the hallway with that one girl I had been digging all night and someone notices us. I hear someone say "What the f--k, we paid for those bitches."
I tell the girl to get in the room with her friend and wait to see who is coming up the stairs. Well of course it's the dickhead that wants to pay for sex.

He gets all up in my face and is upset that he heard I was up here kissing one of the girls while they paid to have these "naked bitches" downstairs servicing them. I tell him to chill out and back up and of course now there are several more of them coming up the stairs.

I make an executive decision: "O.K., I talked to the girls, we can work the price out later. I know you guys are good for it. Give the girls a minute, they're getting set up in the bedroom. Let me go check on them and I'll be right out." I go in the bedroom and lock the door behind me. "Get your shit and climb out the window now!" I say to both of them. "We got to get the f--k out of here. I got all your cash." Luckily we were on the first floor and escape was possible and I figured this was the best thing to do.

All three of us jumped out the window and high tailed it to her car. Someone must have seen us because by the time we were getting into the car the front door opened and dickhead came running at us. Luckily I got it started and punched it fast enough to get out of there without hurting anybody or getting hurt. It was a close.

"If you're going to be a good and faithful judge, you have to resign yourself to the fact that you're not always going to like the conclusions you reach. If you like them all the time, you're probably doing something wrong."

Antonin Scalia

CONCLUSION

Learning the hard way is tough no matter who you are. I remember once breaking up a fight and getting sucker punched that resulted in a fractured eye socket and broken nose. Surgery was $21,000…luckily my workman's compensation covered it. And, I have experienced shots being fired since my guys at the door of one club were armed. I wore a bullet proof vest every shift.

It definitely can be a high risk job. A lot of people get into it for the wrong reasons, ego, pride, women, danger, adrenaline, and partying; they see it as easy money with benefits that can feed personal insecurities and ego. I am a three time convicted felon and recovered drug addict. I learned a lot of hard lessons as I grew up and engaging with this industry has changed me while growing as a person, teacher, businessman and a man. These experiences are now just moments in time to help others make better choices.

For me bouncing was a way to get a reputable security firm, run by an ex law enforcement officer, to notice my skills, see that I was supervisory or management material, and look past my criminal record to offer me a job based on who I am today. All the while, I even took a job bouncing at a rowdy new club that needed regulating. The job only paid $13 an hour and I was already working construction full time and teaching Krav Maga 3 times a week. On top of that, the bar was 70 miles each way from my home. But I did it because I was looking at the big picture, always knew it was a stepping stone for more training opportunities (executive protection) and to build my professional and social resume. I took the risk, got back in the business at age 43 in order to build my resume to get to where I am today, and now I want to help as many people as possible.

While my history has been a tough way to learn valuable lessons, it is my hope to share this book with the intention of helping others be more safe and successful in this line of work. To learn from my experience, how to prepare and be ready is a true goal of this project.

There is a lot within my experience to offer night club owners, bar managers and security personnel today that can really help them avoid unnecessary liability issues, both civilly and criminally. Proper training of security teams and knowing how to find the right people, to implement the highest level of professionalism, is what I can deliver today.

I became a certified Law Enforcement Officer Krav Maga Instructor 5 years ago and just received a letter of recommendation from the director of the police academy here. Currently I am a volunteer with the Sheriff's Department bringing recovery meetings into the county jail every week.

My experience working in nightclubs has been the source of a lot of my success. My current work is training Krav Maga, working with owners, managers and staff, doing community service and working with law enforcement in a training capacity.

Hopefully those reading this book will benefit from my lessons learned and best practices. For the individual who is considering owning, managing or working on a security team at a club or bar, if you have the desire and will, I say go for it!

AFTERWORD
BY BRAM FRANK

This safety and security work isn't for everyone, but everyone in the business needs to understand the vital role safety contributes to their overall success. Gabe Cohen takes the role of a "bouncer" and redefines it for the modern world. Going far beyond the title, this book was a great culmination of philosophy, best practices, strategy, communication, relationships and reality. While the old definition used to create the vision of a huge dude manhandling "bad" clients in a bar, this perspective uses Gabe's successes as the new standard…which required far more than just being a Pit Bull.

Gabe Cohen shows that it's really about leadership, training, teamwork, timing, psychology, being polite until it's time to not be polite, watching out for the legal responsibility and the potential liability of any and all actions. This is a true, comprehensive look at what all owners and security personnel need to consider. These safety and security professionals will interact with the public, protect themselves, clients, the club or bar itself and of course their colleagues. It's certainly NOT about just being a hard-hitting guy and this book delivers the perfect blend of brains and toughness.

Gabe has experienced great lows in his early life and used them to propel himself to great heights as a world class Krav Maga instructor, a good husband, a good father and a man of very strong faith. His approach to being a "bouncer" reflects all of that and more. If I was considering being a bouncer or club owner, this is the guidebook I would want in my hands. Great job!

Bram Frank,
Founder-Grandmaster CSSD/SC
Founder Modular Tactical Systems
Grandmaster Conceptual /Combat Modern Arnis

ABOUT THE AUTHOR

Gabe Cohen is a Black Belt and a certified Law Enforcement Officer Krav Maga Instructor. He has trained and consults with some of the best in the world and has a global presence as a leader in the Krav Maga community. With over 25 years working personal protection and as a security team leader in nightclub risk management, his reputation as the Pitbull Bouncer proceeds him.

Gabe is also the owner of American Krav Maga with affiliates across the United States along with Glenwood Springs Martial Arts Academy. He teaches physical education part time for an elementary school, trains security personnel, does personal protection for celebrities and is available for private instruction.

To learn more about Gabe Cohen visit his website at www.GabeCohenDefense.com, subscribe to his YouTube channel and see him on social media.

Contact Gabe Cohen: Gabe@GabeCohenDefense.com

ABOUT THE AUTHOR

Dave Gerber is a certified Black Belt Instructor of Krav Maga (trained by Martial Arts Masters Hall of Famers Sam Sade and George Buruian) and is the owner of the "L.I.F.E. Line Self-Defense®" system and author of (4) L.I.F.E. Line Self-Defense books for women and children. Dave is also a full instructor under the Patriot Knife System (Thomas Howanic.) Additionally, Dave is a certified leadership coach and a certified Reiki Master. He prides himself on being a life-long learner, having a white belt mentality and a strong desire to help others. He has trained with many of the best and continues to learn each day.

Author of over 10 books, leadership and conflict expert and Master Teacher, Dave has directly trained, coached, facilitated and/or spoken to over 10,000 people at all levels over the last 25 years. He has worked directly with individuals of all ages/backgrounds/abilities and within dozens of different types of organizations. From co-authoring several trainings with NASA and other professional successes to an extensive educational background, Dave offers authentic, profound and transformational results.

Owner of Synergy Development and Training, LLC he works tirelessly to support the efforts of leaders and professionals with authentic, profound and transformative methodologies such as coaching, consulting, training, facilitation, mediation and more. Additionally, his dynamic keynote speaking and "stage presence" has earned him an amazing reputation. "Wisdom not shared is wisdom wasted." To learn more about Dave, please find his books on Amazon, email him directly Gerber@synergydt.com and visit:

www.LifelineSD.com and www.Lifelineselfdefense.com
www.DaveGerber.info and www.DaveGerber.com
www.Synergydt.com

www.pitbullbouncer.com

PITBULL BOUNCER!

A Proven Guide for Nightclub Owners, Bar Managers and Security Personnel!

www.ingramcontent.com/pod-product-compliance
Lightning Source LLC
LaVergne TN
LVHW041625070426
835507LV00008B/456